For My Princess

FALAK

...to whom I was available less during this work

About the Book

For ages, business has been based on physical presence, and physical delivery of goods and services. In e-commerce (electronic commerce), neither physical presence is required nor physical delivery if services are digitized, such as software, videos, books, music and even newspapers and magazines. Suppliers can instead send the products in digital form over the internet, saving both time and cost. Hence, it is difficult to apply the traditional rules of taxation.

E-commerce can be described as the marketing of products that occurs over the internet and mobile. E-commerce is a novel form of marketing which has been developed in conjunction with the ever-growing popularity of the internet and website marketing. Being a relatively new form of marketing in India, majority of corporations continue to market themselves with use of the traditional methods of print magazine advertisements and television commercials.

Goods and Services Tax (GST) was introduced in India from July 1, 2017. GST is a tax on goods and services with comprehensive and continuous chain of set-off benefits up to the retailer level. It is essentially a tax only on value addition at each stage, and a supplier at each stage is permitted to set-off, through a tax credit mechanism, the GST paid on the purchase of goods and services. Ultimately, the burden of GST is borne by the end-user (i.e. final consumer) of the commodity/service. There are special provisions in GST regarding supply of goods or services over digital or electronic network. Government has specified categories of services the tax on which shall be paid by the electronic commerce operator if such services are supplied through him.

This book provides a comprehensive account of the nature of services, e-commerce and its treatment under goods and services tax (GST).

About the Author

Dr. Astha Ahuja is presently Assistant Professor in the Department of Economics, Aryabhatta College, University of Delhi, Delhi. She did her M.A. (Economics) from Jamia Millia Islamia, Delhi and M. Phil. from Delhi School of Economics (DSE), University of Delhi. She received her Ph.D. degree from Jawaharlal Nehru University (JNU), New Delhi. She has authored three books, viz. *Micro, Small and Medium Enterprises (MSMEs) in Post-COVID-19 Era; Agriculture and Rural Development in India: Post-liberalisation Initiatives* and *Value Added Tax: Indian and Global Experiences.*

Dr. Astha worked as Research Associate in the Twelfth Finance Commission in 2003. She also worked as a consultant in Prime Minister's Economic Advisory Council in 2005. She has published a number of articles in leading newspapers and magazines including *Mainstream.*

Foreword

The standard model of development tells us that as countries move up the income ladder, economic activity shifts from agriculture to industry and then on to services after which economies mature into post-industrial societies. India was seen as having defied this text book paradigm by leapfrogging directly from agriculture to services bypassing the industrial stage. We now realize that we need to grow our industrial sector if we are to generate jobs and achieve widely shared prosperity.

This pattern of development reflected in the fiscal dimension. While manufacture was taxed via excise duties and sales via central and state sales tax, services were largely untaxed. Many economists believe that this is one of the factors being India's low tax to GDP ratio.

This anomaly was rectified in stages. Starting the 1990s, both the Centre and states introduced their respective compartmentalized VAT regimes, the Constitution was amended in 2003 to include the right to levy service tax in the Union List which eventually culminated in a unified GST in 2017 under the 'one nation, one tax' principle.

In parallel with India coalescing into a common market, technology has revolutionized the way services are designed, marketed and delivered in ways we never thought possible. Prices of handsets crashed as have prices of internet and telephony allowing for a deep and rapid penetration of digitization. Service providers are able to develop new business models, customize products using big data while user friendly apps have made internet services accessible even to the low income and low literate segments. In particular, many services which required a physical meeting between the provider and consumer are now delivered online and that too more efficiently. E-commerce is now part of our lived experience. Many believe that we are nowhere close to discovering the immense fortune at the bottom of the pyramid.

Astha Ahuja's book *E-commerce and GST in India* dives into this fascinating new world explaining the interconnection between these elements and giving rich insights on how they reinforce each other. It is a valuable contribution to what is still largely a virgin academic area. I wish the book every success.

Hyderabad

Dr. Duvvuri Subbarao
Reserve Bank of India (RBI) Governor
(2008-2013)

Contents

Preface

Marketing is the process of communicating the value of a product or service to customers, for the purpose of selling the product or service. It is a critical business function for attracting customers. Financial success of any organization depends upon marketing ability of that organization. There should be sufficient demand for products and services so the company can make profit. Therefore, many companies created chief marketing officer (CMO) position to put marketing on a more equal footing with other e-level executives.

Good marketing is no accident but a result of careful planning and execution. Marketing practices are continuously being refined to increase the chances of success. However, marketing excellence is rare and difficult to achieve and is an ever expanding task.

New forms of marketing also use the internet and are therefore called *internet marketing* or more generally *e-commerce, online marketing, digital marketing.* Internet marketing is sometimes considered to be broad in scope, because it not only refers to marketing on the Internet, but also includes marketing done via e-mail, wireless media as well as driving audience from traditional marketing methods like radio and billboard to internet properties or landing page.

E-commerce (electronic commerce) can be described as the marketing of the company's products that occurs over the internet and mobile. The objective behind performing electronic marketing is to increase the awareness of a particular company amongst the consumer market.

E-commerce is a novel form of marketing which has been developed in conjunction with the ever-growing popularity of the internet and website marketing. Being a relatively new form of marketing in India, majority of corporations continue to market themselves with use of the traditional methods of print magazine advertisements and television commercials.

Many companies, who are experts in website marketing and

have been conducting business operations over the internet for a couple of years, are aware of electronic marketing and the amazing results in business success it can quickly and effortlessly achieve for them.

Goods and Services Tax (GST) was introduced in India from July 1, 2017. GST is a tax on goods and services with comprehensive and continuous chain of set-off benefits up to the retailer level. It is essentially a tax only on value addition at each stage, and a supplier at each stage is permitted to set-off, through a tax credit mechanism, the GST paid on the purchase of goods and services. Ultimately, the burden of GST is borne by the end-user (i.e. final consumer) of the commodity/service.

Under GST, electronic commerce means the supply of goods or services or both, including digital products over digital or electronic network. Electronic commerce operator means any person who owns, operates or manages digital or electronic facility or platform for electronic commerce. Government has specified categories of services the tax on which shall be paid by the electronic commerce operator if such services are supplied through him.

It may be recalled that during pre-GST era supplying goods through e-commerce platform was not well-defined. Due to differential practices of states in this regard, there was lot of confusion and ambiguity. Under GST, there are clear-cut provisions applicable to e-commerce sector on all-India basis.

I take this opportunity to express my deep gratitude to Professor Arun Kumar who has always been a source of inspiration and encouragement for my academic pursuits. I am highly thankful to Dr. Vinay Kumar, my friend and colleague for making me understand the nuances of corporate finance. I am also thankful to Ms. Mamta Dhasmana and Ms. Jaishree Gupta for their help at every stage of the preparation of this work.

New Delhi
July 2022

Astha Ahuja

1

Features and Marketing of Services

1.1 What are Services?

There exists no precise definition of a service. The term 'service' has been defined differently by researchers and organizations at different points of time. In 1960, American Marketing Association (AMA) defined services as those "activities, benefits or satisfactions which are offered for sale, or provided in connection with the sale of goods". Though this definition was very popular at that time, one major problem with this definition was that it was not able to distinguish between good and services.

A more precise definition of services can be as follows: A service is an activity or series of activities of more or less intangible nature that normally not necessarily, take place in interaction between the customer and service employees and/or physical resources and/or goods and/or system of the service provider which are provided as a solution to customer problem.

Service sector is very wide in its range. It includes, *inter alia*, tourism, trade, hotels, healthcare, education, social security, leasing, entertainment, credit rating agencies, telecommunications, transport, publicity and advertising, insurance, broadcasting, public administration, defence, legal, banking and financial services.

1.1.1 Sub-sectoral Composition of Services Sector: It is as under.

A. Transportation Services: These cover sea, air and others including land, internal waterways, space and pipeline transport services that involve the carriage of passengers, the movement of goods (freight), rentals (charters) of carriers with crew, and related supporting and auxiliary services.

B. Travel and Tourism: It includes goods and services

acquired by personal travellers for health, education or other purposes, and by business travellers. Unlike other services, travel is not a specific type of service, but an assortment of goods and services consumed by travellers. The most common goods and services covered are lodging, food and beverages, entertainment and transportation, gifts and souvenirs.

C. Computer and Information Services: These include computer services (hardware and software related services and data processing services), news agency services, and other information provision services.

D. Other Business Services: These comprise trade-related services, operational leasing (rentals), and miscellaneous business, professional and technical services such as legal, accounting, management consulting, public relations services, advertising, market research and public opinion polling, research and deployment services, architectural, engineering, and other technical services.

1.2 Characteristics of Services

The marketing as well as services marketing literature recognize services as being different in nature from products. Services have some distinguishing characteristics which differentiate them from goods. A brief discussion of these characteristics and their implications to services marketers is as follows:

1.2.1 Intangibility: The literature highlights intangibility as one of the key characteristics of services. Services are essentially intangible in nature and as such do not possess material form, and thus cannot be touched, seen, heard, tasted, or smelled. This has an important implication for the marketers in the sense that they cannot tell in advance to the customers as to what they will be getting. Unless the institutions supplying them have a good image and confidence among the customers, they may face difficulties in seeking customers' shares of mind and wallets. Service quality goes a long way in building favourable images in the minds of customers. The service marketers, therefore, have to focus on quality of their services to build their credibility and gain trust of the clients.

1.2.2 Inseparability: Services are referred to as being inseparable because services are delivered and consumed simultaneously and as such cannot be separated from the service provider. Since consumers are mostly present at the time of service delivery, they tend to affect or shape the performance and quality of service. Provision of good quality service, therefore, requires proper management of not only the employees, but also of customers so as to ensure that the interactions between the two are productive and capable of generating good quality service.

The use of a service is inherently subjective, meaning that several persons experiencing a service would each experience it uniquely. For example, a metro ride can be deemed a service. If one buys a metro ticket, the use of the metro is typically experienced concurrently with the purchase of the ticket. Although the metro is a physical object, one is not paying for the permanent ownership of the tangible components of the metro.

1.2.3 Heterogeneity: Services involve people, and people are all different. If not managed properly, service performance can differ not only from person to person, but also for a given person from day to day. There is, for instance, a strong possibility that the same enquiry would be answered slightly differently by different people (or even by the same person at different times). In other words, heterogeneity reflects the potential for high variability in service delivery and quality.

1.2.4 Perishability: In general, services cannot be stored and carried forward to a future time period. In simple words, perishability means inability to produce service in advance and store it for future use. For example, vacant seats on an airplane cannot be transferred to the next flight. In a similar vein, query-free times at the reference desk cannot be saved up until there is a busy period. Services are "time dependent" and "time important" which make them very perishable. Apart from requiring proper demand management, the perishabillity characteristic of services entails an important implication from the point of view of quality management. This is so, because while goods can be produced in advance and inventoried for future sale, this is not possible with services. Services in general are produced and delivered simultaneously or immediately as and when demanded by the customers, and these are as such not amenable to pre-delivery quality controls as is the case with the goods.

1.2.5 Services as a Spectrum: Services (compared with goods) can also be viewed as a spectrum. Not all products are either pure goods or pure services. An example would be a restaurant, where a waiter's service is intangible, but the food is tangible.

These characteristics of services make evaluation and purchase of services a difficult task for the consumers.

1.3 Marketing of Services

Since services are acts, deeds and performances performed by people, the role of human resources in the marketing services is important. It may be mentioned here that in the context of services, people include not only the employees but also the customers. Service quality is dependent on the interactions between the service provider and receiver. Management of the employees is important because customers' evaluation of service is depends on the specialized skills, competencies, techniques and experience of employees which, in turn, influence customers' perception of service quality and their satisfaction. Customers also need to be managed because many a time they are also co-producers of the service and they need to co-operate with the service employees for effective delivery of services. If not managed properly, some of the customers may turn out to be rowdy, thus affecting the serenity of the service space and spoil the mood of other customers as well as of contact service staff.

Then, there is a set of procedures and policies that are

prescribed by the firm for the service staff to follow for executing service transactions. These procedures are laid down with a view to standardize the service acts and also to ensure performance of all the steps or tasks as are necessary for a complete, safe and efficient transaction. Proper understanding and utilization of service process can go a long way in improving the quality of service, both directly and indirectly. Poorly developed service processes and blueprints, on the other hand, can severely affect customer perceptions about service quality.

Physical evidence is another key determinant of customer service quality perceptions. Physical evidence refers to physical environment and other tangibles associated with the service such as land and building, parking space, furniture, machinery and office equipments, signages, employees' uniform, lighting conditions and ventilation. These artefacts and their layout help not only in tangibalising the intangibles and thus directly affecting the service quality perceptions, but also indirectly by way of enabling the employees to perform better and the customers to be in a better mood to receive the services.

1.4 Importance of Quality of Services

Maintaining high level of quality is not the philosophy, but an essential product requirement for providing satisfaction to the customers and making them loyal to the firm. Today's consumers are well educated and can easily access information from a wide variety of sources. They are quite knowledgeable of their rights and do not hesitate taking actions against companies which fail to honour their promises. Many consumers today are also ready to pay higher prices to get better product quality.

Higher quality helps organization to achieve its objectives of obtaining higher market share, higher sales turnover, higher return on investment etc. It is precisely in recognition of the need for higher quality to the consumers, that many international and national organizations have come up to provide quality accreditation such as ISO certificate to companies which take necessary steps in providing quality products and services to the consumers.

There is no single definition that covers all the aspects of service quality. Considering service quality as an all embracing term, it can be defined as a bundle of attributes such as performance, features, conformance, reliability, durability, aesthetics and serviceability.

1.5 Economic Development and Services Sector

Occupational classification refers to the distribution of available occupations in a country into meaningful categories. In general, all occupations are broadly divided into three categories:

1. Primary sector (agriculture and allied activities).
2. Secondary sector (industrial activities).
3. Tertiary sector (services sector).

Occupational structure refers to the distribution of working persons across primary sector, secondary sector and tertiary sector. There is a close relationship between economic development and occupational structure of a country. A higher per capita income country is always associated with a higher proportion of the working population employed in tertiary sector. Contrarily, a low per capita income country is always associated with a higher proportion of working population engaged in agriculture.

In the preliminary stage of economic growth, the proportion of the work force engaged in the agricultural and allied occupations is high. As the economy grows, the share of working population in primary sector declines and that of secondary and tertiary sectors increases. At high levels of economic development, the share of tertiary sector is more than that in secondary sector. Economic development is associated with a relative shift in the structure of the work force away from agriculture, towards industry and services.

1.6 Taxation of Services

From equity point of view, services should be taxed in the same way as goods. Taxation of goods and exclusion of services distorts the relative prices of goods vis-à-vis services, encouraging artificially the demand for services. In the process, the allocation of resources is also distorted. If tax is imposed on goods and not on services, a relatively high rate of tax would be required on goods to generate a given amount of revenue. If tax is imposed both on goods and services, a moderate tax rate can yield the given revenue. Administratively, taxation of both goods and services is desirable because it would reduce disputes pertaining to distinction between goods and services.

1.7 Tourism: A Leading Service

1.7.1 Why is Tourism Important? Tourism sector has a major role to play to promote faster, sustainable and more inclusive economic growth. It has better prospects for promoting pro-poor growth than many other sectors. This is because tourism involves a collection of activities, services and industries comprising transportation, accommodation, eating and drinking establishments, retail shops, entertainment businesses and other hospitality services provided to individuals or groups travelling away from home for leisure, business or other purposes. The broad scope of economic activities involved enables wide participation in its growth, including participation by the informal sector. Tourism is also highly dependent upon natural capital (mountains, forests, rivers, lakes, wildlife) and culture and these are assets that some of the poor have, even if they have no financial resources. For all these reasons, across the world, the tourism industry is one of the largest generators of employment.

In India, the tourism sector is based on exploiting its unique endowments of biodiversity, forests, rivers, and its rich culture and heritage. The challenges in this sector lie in successfully preserving these in their original form, and making them accessible to domestic and international travellers. Tourism in

India has the potential to create economic interest of local communities in the protection of its natural and cultural endowments leading to a more *sustainable growth.*

1.7.2 Travel and Tourism Competitiveness Report 2019: In the *Travel and Tourism Competitiveness Report 2019* published by the World Economic Forum, India was placed at 34th position among 140 countries of the world. India showed the greatest percentage improvement to its overall score, helping it to become the only low-middle income country in the top 35.

India was ranked at 52nd place (among 141 countries) in the 2015 Report and at 40th place (among 136 countries) in the 2017 Report. Thus, India jumped 18 spots in 4 years (from 52nd in 2015 to 34th in 2019) and 6 spots in 2 years (from 40th in 2017 to 34th in 2019).

Cultural heritage and natural resources are, expectedly, two factors where India scores highly in the Report. The country also worked on its business environment and environmental sustainability.

1.7.3 Sustainable Tourism: While tourism is important for both growth and employment generation, it must also be sustainable. The World Tourism Organization (WTO) has defined sustainable tourism as 'leading to management of all resources in such a way that economic, social and aesthetic needs can be fulfilled while maintaining cultural integrity, essential ecological processes, biological diversity and life support systems'. In 1992, the Earth Summit in Rio established the triple principles of environmental, economic and social sustainability. Since then, the principles of sustainable tourism have been adopted by the tourism industry worldwide.

The traditional approach to tourism development is a direct result of an extremely open and deregulated world economic environment. This approach is characterised by inequity in redistribution of economic benefits. Over the years, new non-traditional approaches (like eco-tourism) which are concerned more with ecological and cultural conservation than poverty reduction have become popular. The aim is more on minimizing costs on people's lives rather than bringing benefits to them.

1.7.4 Pro-poor Tourism: Any strategy to promote tourism should emphasise the need to adopt a *pro-poor tourism* approach aimed at increasing the net benefits to the poor from tourism and ensure that tourism growth contributes to poverty reduction. The benefits may be economic, social, environmental or cultural. For this purpose, there is a need for developing a comprehensive set of strategies for a diversity of actions, from micro to macro level, including product and infrastructure development, marketing, branding and promotion, planning, policy and investment and increasing the spread of benefits to the weaker sections.

To realize the tourism potential of India's enormous assets—namely historical sites, places of religious significance, and its vast range of national attractions—the focus must be on developing clusters or circuits around such assets. The development of these clusters/circuits requires collaboration between many agencies at the local level to create an attractive and safe transit experience. Therefore, development of tourism requires that States take a leading role in developing their own tourism potential to obtain growth in employment and income.

1.7.5 Tourism Infrastructure: Availability of good infrastructure is one of the essential requirements at selected tourist destinations. Infrastructure for tourism includes as under:

1. Travel infrastructure networks like airports, railways, roads, waterways, and telecommunications.
2. Amenities like electricity, water supply, drainage, sewerage, solid waste disposal systems.
3. Tourism facilities, services and amenities like accommodation, restaurants, recreational facilities and shopping facilities.

The operation of tourism facilities, services and amenities are often dependent on a number of travel infrastructure networks. The most usual case in tourism development is for infrastructure development to precede the completion of the tourism facilities. This means that the installation of the infrastructure becomes a public sector responsibility. The case for infrastructure services being a public sector responsibility is based on the consideration that the network of services is available to both tourists and residents of the area *and* the construction of an integrated system would also facilitate non-tourism development within the region.

The strategy for development of tourism infrastructure should essentially focus on identifying clusters of habitations and destinations having unique craft, ethnic art form, culture and heritage, natural spots for development as tourism products and develop tourist circuits/destinations around them with the active participation of local communities. As part of this strategy, State Governments should be expected to identify at least *one integrated tourist circuit*, map all the tangible and intangible natural and cultural assets along the circuit, estimate the sustainable destination carrying capacity and undertake a gap analysis of the travel infrastructure network and tourism facilities, services and amenities.

Based on this, a comprehensive integrated physical and financial plan should be prepared through a community participatory process. The plan should identify, *inter alia*, the winners and losers, agencies responsible for executing the sub-components of the plan and the timelines for achieving the milestones. The integrated plan should be approved and monitored by the Ministry of Tourism.

Easy access to tourism destinations in terms of international transport and facilities for easy movement within the destinations are prerequisites for the development of tourism. India's ability to open up new areas and properly service emerging tourism resorts, while also providing access to natural tourism attractions and circuits for tours will significantly depend upon its ability to quickly improve the airport density and quality of rail and roads.

In terms of investment, especially private investment, tourist accommodation represents the most expensive facility in tourist resorts. In the past few decades, the character and composition of tourist accommodation has undergone considerable change. New types of accommodation, such as self-catering units, home stay, budget hotel accommodation and camping sites, have evolved to meet market demands for increased levels of independence, self-sufficiency, informality, economy and convenience. Such changes have been influenced by the emergence of the new types of travellers and the tourists who invest in a holiday home or unit in a preferred tourism destination. As the spectrum of travellers has undergone transformation, there have also been changes in requirements for traditional hotel accommodation.

The availability of hotel rooms in India is extremely limited. Further, there is acute shortage of land in urban areas particularly in cities due to land market distortions. Therefore, the prospect of large-scale new traditional hotel accommodation is extremely limited. It is imperative to expand the number of registrations under the home stay scheme in various stays so as to significantly augment hotel room capacity in India. This will open up new livelihood opportunities for local people.

1.7.6 Human Resources Development for Tourism:

As in some other service sectors there is a large skill deficit in the tourism sector, which is impeding its development and impinging on its competitiveness.

The Indian Institute of Travel and Tourism Management (IITTM) is an institute affiliated to the All India Council for Technical Education, running courses for tour operators and holding examinations and granting diploma. The IITTM also conducts short-term courses for tour guides, holds examinations and grants diplomas for the profession.

Tourism is a labour-intensive industry and a major source of employment. Therefore, issues of human resources development and capacity building are extremely important. The problem of human resources is identified as a shortage of trained labour; lack of trainers; inadequate training materials and lack of tourism education strategies as part of national tourism planning. Other issues concerning human resources development in the tourism industry include: working conditions, availability of education and training, policy issues, information and technology and cultural issues.

Developing human resources in the tourism sector faces unique challenges because customer preferences, travel patterns, information technology and conditions at destinations are changing rapidly. As a result, strong and flexible human resources development strategies are needed. The strategy should mirror human resources needs and the corresponding recruitment, employment and training requirements.

Training programmes need to articulate well with employment creation, for maximum synergy. Training should be strictly need-based. Thus, it is necessary to establish linkages with various labour market institutions and processes: labour market information, employment services, public works, credit and other support to small enterprises, unemployment and social support services and so on. Training services for existing enterprises to upgrade and re-orient technical skills or develop management capacity can help stimulate their labour absorption, avoid retrenchments and facilitate redeployment of retrenched workers. Therefore, the tourism training strategy should focus on employability, sustainability and promotion of decent work culture especially to safeguard foreign tourists.

1.7.7 Tourist Clusters: In the affluent countries there is flow of tourists out of the cities not only during holidays and almost every weekend, weather permitting. The weekend tourists, particularly those with children, normally go out short distances to resorts and tourist destinations, such as mountains, lakes and beaches. But they also go to man made attractions and clusters of attractions such as Santosa Island Resort in Singapore.

Rapid increase in disposable income in the upper middle class in India presents a big opportunity for development of tourism in the country.

Efforts should be made for the creation of tourism clusters of areas between 100 and 500 acres within a distance of 150 kilometres for the cities for the setting up of a cluster of facilities and attractions for tourism. They may have hotels, restaurants, spas, theme parks like Appu Ghar in Delhi and Essel World in Mumbai, and attractions such as skating rinks, lakes with boating and sailing facilities, golf courses, tennis courts, and indoor games. Although the clientele of tourist clusters will primarily be domestic, they will also serve to increase the attractiveness of traditional tourist destinations for international tourists.

1.7.8 Tourism Products in India: Tourism in India has an impressive variety of tourism products:

1. Heritage and culture tourism (with 26 World Heritage Sites).
2. Eco-tourism (wild life in National Parks).
3. Adventure tourism (mountain climbing, mountain trekking, river-based sports including rafting, and skiing).
4. Wellness tourism (ayurveda and yoga institutes in Kerala and Rishikesh) and medical tourism (being developed by private sector hospital chains).
5. Beach tourism (centred around Goa).
6. Religious tourism (Varanasi, Haridwar, Tirupati, Bodh Gaya, Ajmer, Amritsar).
7. MICE (meetings, incentives, conferences and exhibitions) tourism.
8. Desert tourism.
9. Rural tourism.

Undoubtedly tourism in India has a remarkable variety and contributes substantially to the economy, particularly in providing jobs, full time or part time. Growth in international tourist arrivals during recent years has been significant. International tourism has also provided sustenance to the Indian handicrafts industry (carpets and other handcrafted textile products; brassware; inlaid marble and rosewood; bidri; papier mache etc.).

Beaches are one of the most important destinations for the affluent tourists. India has a coastline of 6,000 kilometres but beach tourism is not well developed, Goa being the only international beach destination in the country. One factor, which affects the competitiveness of beach tourism in India, is the stringent coastal regulations zone requirements (CRZ), under which a hotel cannot be built within 200 metres of the coast. Such a restriction does not exist in any successful beach destination in the world.

Meetings, incentives, conferences and exhibitions (MICE) is another area of tourism in which India lacks in competitiveness because of lack of world class conference centre apart from Delhi's Vigyan Bhawan, which is normally reserved for Government conferences.

Whether it is heritage tourism or beach tourism, the foreign tourists as well as domestic leisure travellers want some form of entertainment, particularly in the evening. For this purpose, consideration needs to be given to allowing casinos to operate in certain locations. Though the subject has remained a taboo in the country it has to be borne in mind that casinos will not only increase the competitiveness of tourism destinations in the country but also have the potential to generate substantial revenues for the State Governments, just as lotteries have done for some of them. Casinos are the mainstay of the economies of tourist destinations such as Las Vegas, Monte Carlo and Macau. Singapore too has allowed the establishment of two casinos in its territory.

1.7.9 Centre-State Co-ordination: In terms of the federal framework of the Constitution, the responsibilities of the Union Government and the State Governments are elaborated in separate schedules to the Constitution.

The Central Government is responsible for matters such as external affairs, visa regulations, foreign exchange regulations and import/export procedures, while the State Governments are responsible, inter alia, for law and order, land use, civic amenities, shops and establishments. These Governments have separate agencies for dealing with specific subjects and regulations. For example, the Ministry of Tourism in the

Union Government is concerned with the overall coordination and planning of tourism development in the country and for undertaking tourism promotion and publicity in the international market.

However, the State Governments control all factors of production including land in their territories. Further, there is empirical evidence to suggest that a significant proportion of their tax revenues are attributable to consumption by tourists. Therefore, the State Governments have the responsibility and the incentive for facilitating the creation of infrastructure for tourism. The role of the Union Government is restricted to establishing a policy and regulatory framework, creating the appropriate incentive structure and synergising the activities of different infrastructure sectors across levels of government and supplementing these efforts by financial assistance.

1.7.10 Impediments to Tourism in India: The paucity of tourist accommodation, inadequate transportation arrangements made expensive by deficient infrastructure and taxation, inadequate development of tourist destinations, which are bereft of ambience and lacking in amenities for tourists and facilities for their entertainment are some of the major impediments. One aspect that is becoming increasingly relevant is the sheer shortage of places of entertainment within a motorable distance of cities where families may go for leisure purposes for weekends. Most of the hill stations in both North and South India are highly overcrowded during the season and is avoided by the tourist class that has the a large disposable income. There are other more specific problems also and we take them all up in turn.

A. Air Transport: A few years ago non-availability of seats on flights to and from India deterred international tourists and the high domestic fares were a handicap for leisure travellers within the country. The position has eased considerably and with the progressive liberalization of bilateral agreements and introduction of open skies policy there is better availability of seats on international flights. The process of liberalization must continue in order to increase: (a) direct international connectivity with non-metro destinations and (b) direct air connectivity with long haul overseas markets. The entry of low cost domestic carriers has improved access to air travel within the country as well and eventually could lead to opening up new areas to tourism in India such as the North-East.

B. Road Transport: A large number of foreign and domestic tourists use dedicated tourist vehicles mainly buses for visiting tourist destinations and the private sector has made large investments in these vehicles. The road and passenger tax regimes of the State Governments increase the cost of travel but more importantly they are a source of harassment to the tourists because of the manner of their implementation. Some States charge taxes on a quarterly basis, some per day and others on a per seat basis, which could be in addition to the quarterly charges. The buses carrying tourists have to stop at the borders for long periods every trip as the papers are checked and taxes collected where necessary. Even if the quarterly or daily taxes have been paid there is no respite from standing in the queue along with other such vehicles and trucks. The problem is exacerbated by the limited and over worked staff.

C. Maintenance of Heritage Sites: The Archaeological Survey of India (ASI) has the responsibility for the maintenance and upkeep of all monuments and archaeological sites notified by the Government of India as a protected monument under the Ancient Monuments and Archaeological Sites and Remains Act, 1958. Some of the States have also enacted similar legislation and notified monuments and archaeological sites under the Acts. The allocation of funds made available to the ASI is grossly inadequate for the maintenance and restoration of the monuments and the environs of these monuments. The difference that adequate funds can make to a monument has been well illustrated by the case of Humayun Tomb in New Delhi, which has been transformed with the help of donations from the Agha Khan Foundation. Paucity of funds is also a contributory factor for the present state of neglect in which the Delhi Red Fort finds itself.

The position is not very different in the case of monuments protected by the State Governments. In a large number of monuments not even minimum facilities such as provision of drinking water and toilets has been provided.

As a highly labour-intensive sector, tourism has the capacity to generate large-scale, good quality employment. The sector has multiple forward and backward linkages with further job generating potential in sectors such as agriculture, retail, transport and financial services.

Recognizing the sector's potential to generate income and employment, the government has undertaken several measures to strengthen infrastructure and facilitate tourism. India recently introduced tourist visa on arrival, enabled with electronic travel authorization (ETA) (renamed as e-Tourist Visa) for tourists from 150 countries. The Ministry of Tourism has launched a round-the-clock, toll-free tourist helpline in 12 international languages. The Government has launched several schemes to:

1. Develop tourist circuits.
2. Develop islands as tourist destinations.
3. Build large-scale convention centres in different cities.
4. Improve connectivity.
5. Develop niche offerings such as medical tourism and pilgrimage-based tourism.

2

Marketing and E-commerce

2.1 Importance of Marketing

Marketing is the process of communicating the value of a product or service to customers, for the purpose of selling the product or service. It is a critical business function for attracting customers.

Financial success of any organization depends upon marketing ability of that organization. There should be sufficient demand for products and services so the company can make profit. Therefore, many companies created chief marketing officer (CMO) position to put marketing on a more equal footing with other e-level executives.

Good marketing is no accident but a result of careful planning and execution. Marketing practices are continuously being refined to increase the chances of success. However, marketing excellence is rare and difficult to achieve and is an ever expanding task.

From a societal point of view, marketing is the link between a society's material requirements and its economic patterns of response. Marketing satisfies these needs and wants through exchange processes and building long-term relationships. It is the process of communicating the value of a product or service through positioning to customers. Marketing can be looked at as an organizational function and a set of processes for creating, delivering and communicating value to customers, and managing customer relationships in ways that also benefit the organization and its shareholders. Marketing is the science of choosing target markets through market analysis and market segmentation, as well as understanding consumer buying behaviour and providing superior customer value.

Marketing, whether to consumers or to business, has a well

defined purpose in most organizations. That purpose is to create exchanges that satisfy consumer and organizational goals. As marketing strategy is constructed to address a particular product/market, two tasks must be performed by elements of the marketing mix: the communications task and the operating task.

The communication task can be thought of as information, primarily conveyed through promotion, price, the product label and package. This information is used to position the product in the market and to inform and/or persuade present or potential customers. The operating task is to remove barriers to transactions or exchanges so that customers who perceive the product as being capable of satisfying their needs and preferences can engage in a transaction with minimum effort. These barriers center around the following:

1. Product accessibility.
2. Product availability.
3. Owning/using the product.
4. Correct perception and recall.
5. Differential utility.

The operating task has traditionally been implemented so that the transaction is enhanced by having the right product or service at the right place at the right time with the right service and the customer can take possession. A marketer, to execute these communication and operating tasks, uses one or more channels. The emergence of a new channel, i.e. internet has great impact on consumer marketing. There are two important aspects of consumer marketing that the internet is capable of transforming: (a) the communication process, and (b) the consumer need fulfilment through new processes.

2.1.1 Consumer Centricity of Business: Stakeholder engagement has evolved with the changing role of corporations in the society. It has changed from being a reaction to customer problems to their greater participation in the value chain. The stakeholder engagement has benefited many companies through informed decision-making by generating business intelligence. It also brings diverse perspectives together for creativity and innovation.

Earlier, through traditional means of marketing, there used to be a monologue between customers and businesses and a wide range of advertisement was broadcasted. But the modern customer has less time to watch all these advertisements and therefore chooses the message he wishes to see. As internet facilitates interactions, customers want that companies should listen to them and respond. Technology is serving in a big way by helping companies get insights about their customers. Companies are offering customized products and services to their customers as they are no longer the passive players in the market. They already have a lot of information at their disposal. Therefore, being customer centric is the only way to survive in the modern day markets.

The concept of *digital customer engagement* emphasizes the dependence and reliability on customer generated content. Online modes of consumer engagement are gaining popularity as they involve internet marketing, social media marketing, blogs, web portals, crowd sourcing, e-mail campaigns etc and have wide number of applications in different sectors. Many private companies are now using social media platforms, mobile devices and other technologies to get closer to their customers because of their volume and speed to reach customers.

Technology has also changed the way customers contact the companies. They seek automation, self-service and personalization. The technology also brings good prospects for the government and the jurisdiction of the country as it helps them to empower the citizens and gives them more access to the details through the use of location-based services. It helps in achieving long-term operational efficiencies.

As mobile phones (now mostly smart phones) have become an integral part of our day-to-day life, there is a need to change the way businesses reach and interact with its customers. Smart phones act as primary internet devices and thus can be used for mass marketing to gain more participation. To ensure deeper reach, the focus must be on developing customer-centric applications. There is a need to make these applications available in different languages to avoid the gap that may be generated. Some touch points that can be of core importance for the businesses to engage with customers through mobiles are product discovery platforms, search engines, customer care portals, consumer grievance forums and digital payment mechanisms.

The proliferation of social media and the video invasion are instrumental for building strong relationships with customers. Videos ensure attention for longer duration and provide opportunities for emotional congruence. Social media relationships build on videos and social interaction results in self-efficacy and positive word of mouth. Social interactions and shared experiences increase the levels of commitment and engagement with the businesses. Increased interaction results in more satisfied customers and thereby positive actions. To attain higher levels of consumer engagement, businesses must integrate the digital channels with traditional brick and mortar.

Finally, to be a customer-centric company, a collective effort by different departments of the organization is an imperative practice. It is unlike product-centric approach where the functions are compartmentalized. Linkages have to be developed across the organization and a better understanding of customer needs has to be discovered at every level. These linkages are being made with the help of internet technologies. Even customers should be treated as business partners and their feedback and suggestions should be taken into consideration. E-tailers must first ask consumers what they want to buy rather than trying to push what they want to sell.

2.1.2 Marketing and Advertising: Companies use various marketing tools to increase customer engagement and participation. Internet has become much more user-friendly with the passage of time. Online business activities are a rapidly growing phenomenon. Internet has proved to be a powerful medium for obtaining and distributing information to help marketers take product decisions and devise appropriate marketing plans.

As the popularity of internet has increased, the popularity of sports has increased as well. Viewers are no more glued to their TV screens, wishing to watch only live shows. They want the convenience of watching their favourite matches whenever and wherever they want to. Digitization of media content, proliferation of IT-enabled devices and easy availability of high speed broadband connections has given birth to the phenomenon called *media convergence*—a phenomenon involving the interconnection of information and communications technologies, computer networks, and media content. Various forms of media such as TV, social platforms and even out-of-home (OoH) advertising, are being used by brands to bridge the gap between online and offline resources. It helps them to efficiently identify their target group of sports fans.

Sports fans are some of the most loyal customers because they are open to use the products of the brands, which are participating in their favourite games. Brands not only need to provide relevant content and enhanced experience to the sports fans, but also engage them sustainably with the brand. Programmatic technology is the need of the hour. Here, with the help of triggers, ads and content can be displayed to the viewers based on monitoring real time developments as the game progresses.

OoH advertising is an old form of advertising which was assumed to be restricted to hoardings and billboards on roadsides. They were more of a distraction rather than attention gainers. Now IT has shown the way to modernize the OoH advertising in the form of digitized and interactive billboards. OoH advertising has shown good results in the rural markets as well. In rural areas, people gather at public places such as bus stops or marketplaces, where many OoH exercises like permanent billboards are done. Even though the quality of those billboards is very basic, they have proven to be better communication tools than most others.

2.2 Advent of Internet

With the commercialization of the internet, the nature of society has changed in many ways. In recent years, the economic power of internet has grown and further reconfigured the world we live in. Today, internet can be seen as a platform that assists in continuous technological innovations, encourages new business practices and changes the competitive landscape of various industry sectors. With technological innovations, internet has changed from *publishing-browsing-platform* to a *participation-interaction-platform*. It has enabled new business models and fostered changes in social life.

Researchers have clearly identified internet as a platform that cannot be overlooked or ignored by tourism organizations while forming their marketing mixes owing to its advantages such as global accessibility, convenience in updating, real time information service, interactive communication features and unique customization capabilities. Internet is successful in swift identification of customer needs and establishment of direct contact with consumers, offering them comprehensive, personalized and up-to-date information. Tourism suppliers can remotely control their servers to display information on products/services at an electronic speed. As far as the travellers are concerned, internet allows them to communicate directly with tourism suppliers to seek information. It also empowers them to develop and purchase their own itineraries anytime and anywhere.

Internet services are regarded as catalyst in the growth of an economy. Since the information system of a country is interconnected, the development and deployment of information and communication technology is crucial for expanding knowledge base and increasing productivity. Development of technologies and improvement in telecommunications infrastructure has enabled loosely bound business entities to collaborate and provide a number of services, thus connecting more communities socially as well as technologically.

Broadband internet connection is a powerful tool for business enterprises as it provides connectivity to the global markets at a much lower cost than ever. It also acts as an enabling technology that allows them to adopt a number of valuable complimentary applications that may increase their efficiency.

The growth of the internet during the past few years is undoubtedly the most important development in the history of commerce which shows no signs of abating in the future. Since the Industrial Revolution of the 19th century, no development has so dramatically altered human behaviour as the emergence of internet. Marketing has also been immensely influenced by the Internet. Marketers have got a new medium for communicating and building long-term relationship with their customers at a fraction of cost they used to incur earlier. Various marketing activities can be performed more efficiently, effectively and smoothly than ever before with the help of internet. However, it is difficult to assess the potential of internet for business and foresee the probable threats brought by the new medium.

In India, the internet became available to the general public and the business in 1995. People have been mesmerized by the prowess of the internet, both as a communication tool and as an entertainment medium. The Indian corporate world was quick to realize the commercial potential of the Web and embraced it as part of its business and marketing strategies. The Indian Government has also been providing the necessary infrastructural support for the internet. Worldwide, and in India also, empirical studies are being conducted to explore the possibilities of doing business on the internet, including growth in the volume of e-commerce, use of websites, online pricing and online advertising. However, what marketers in India think about the internet as a marketing tool and how they can use it for marketing purposes has not been attempted in a systematic manner.

2.3 Internet Marketing and E-commerce

New forms of marketing also use internet and are therefore

called *internet marketing* or more generally *e-commerce, online marketing, digital marketing.* Internet marketing is sometimes considered to be broad in scope, because it not only refers to marketing on the internet, but also includes marketing done via email, wireless media as well as driving audience from traditional marketing methods like radio and billboard to internet properties or landing page.

E-commerce (electronic commerce) can be described as the marketing of the company's products that occurs over the internet and mobile. The objective behind performing electronic marketing is to increase the awareness of a particular company amongst the consumer market.

E-commerce is a novel form of marketing which has been developed in conjunction with the ever-growing popularity of the internet and website marketing. Being a relatively new form of marketing in India, majority of corporations continue to market themselves with use of the traditional methods of print magazine advertisements and television commercials.

Many companies, who are experts in website marketing and have been conducting business operations over the internet for a couple of years, are aware of electronic marketing and the amazing results in business success it can quickly and effortlessly achieve for them.

2.3.1 Risk and Trust: Trust plays an important role in e-commerce activities. Trust is an important factor for the circulation and acceptance of e-commerce. There are two types of uncertainty, namely system-dependent and transaction specific. Online retailers are finding it increasingly difficult to sell their goods. Internet users are unwilling to shop online because of lack of faith that must exist between business and consumers. Trust is not only a short-term issue but the most important long-term barrier to realize the full potential of e-commerce. Consumers foresee numerous risks while buying on the internet as it does not involve simultaneous exchange of goods and money, because of the temporal separation between exchange partners.

System dependent uncertainties arise because of potential technological problems and lack of clear legal norms. On the other hand, transaction-specific uncertainties arise out of asymmetric distribution of information between the transaction partners. Trust plays a key role in buying process as consumers tend to look for experience in credence qualities of products and their sellers. Trust functions to lower the perceived risk of a transaction. On the other hand, there are some risks that come about during exchange of information via internet.

System-dependent uncertainty comprises of events that are beyond the direct influence of actors and can be characterized as environmental uncertainty. In the context of the internet, it relates to potential technological sources of errors and security gaps.

Technical safety gaps can emerge either in the data channel or on the final points of the process like the desktop system of the customer, the server of the internet retailer or the involved banks. Transaction specific uncertainty may arise out of decisions of economic actors and is caused by asymmetric distribution of information between the transaction partners. This primarily concerns the quality of products and services offered on the web because the quality assessment in electronic markets is much more difficult due to disappearance of the personal factors that are used in traditional modes of selling. This type of uncertainty can be reduced by application of concepts of search, experience and credence qualities. Online product evaluation is possible through performance-oriented information substitutes that relate to the seller and his reputation in the market or adequate indicators such as brand names or performance bonds.

Online retailers facilitate the evaluation of credence qualities by signalling trustworthiness like referring to a certificate of a trusted third party. Trust is a potentially important aspect for reducing uncertainty and complexity of online transactions and relationships. Trust is considerably useful in reaping economic benefits. Since in the near future trust will remain the decisive factor for success or failure of e-businesses, it is very important for internet companies to act in a way that engenders consumers' trust. Efforts to increase the security of e-commerce systems and trustworthy behaviour of online retailers will prove to be of advantage for both consumers and companies engaging in e-commerce.

2.3.2 Websites Shopping: There has been a phenomenal growth in the number of organizations using internet for marketing, promoting, and transacting products and services because of growth in B2C e-commerce. Firms and consumers have started using internet to gather information and for online shopping. The usefulness of a B2C site not only depends upon the content and design but also the navigation tools. There has been much technical advancement in internet security including cryptography, digital signatures, and certificates and authentication. Despite these advancements, consumers are apprehensive about online shopping. An effective B2C site provides quick access to information about product and services, information about the organization (the seller) and contact information.

A substantial number of customers experience problems while shopping online such as lost orders, service breakdowns, or inadequate handling of complaints. All these problems make the maintenance of the quality of e-service challenging.

Online shopping experience is different from offline shopping experience. There are many factors affecting online purchasing behaviour of consumer such as attitude towards technology, skills and experiences, people having greater internal control, knowledge of internet, willingness to adopt new technology or those who spend much of their time online, are more likely to shop online. Furthermore, those who are time starved are more likely to shop online.

Other factors also influence the decision of shopping online or offline, such as type of product, customer mood and goal behind shopping. It is also found that website design, reliability and security/privacy serve as the basis of judgment for the quality of an online site. As more and more information and technological tools are available to customers, their preferences and experiences are likely to change.

2.3.3 Travelling Displacement: In the times of internet, the need for business travel may get eliminated. Internet allows business and people to call, email, see and talk to counterparties without travelling to distant locations. Most of the business travel relates to management of foreign subsidiaries. The brain needs to move and not the bytes, primarily because:

1. Brain has a capacity to absorb information, identify patterns and solve problems without us being aware of how it does it. It lets us understand facial expressions, body language, intonation and other subtle indicators that are gathered unconsciously and results in better evaluation.
2. Brain is designed to work in parallel with other brains.

Thus, it is noted that the amount of travel is related to the amount of know-how that needs to be moved around. Thus, it is suggested that firms must try to move brains for key tasks and not just for relevant information to the brains.

E-commerce is also a major use, especially when making purchases, downloading software, financial transactions, placing product service requests, and downloading music are considered together.

Internet use leads to trip substitution as many use information technology instead of making trips to work, bookstores, other stores, and libraries. Information technology is also frequently used instead of making trips to clothing stores, music stores, friends' houses, government offices, and special interest organizations.

Internet is used to gather information to prompt trips to bookstores, other stores, government offices, movies, libraries, and other stores.

3

Evolution and Approaches to E-commerce

Commerce has evolved over the years. Prior to the evolution of money, it was a simple barter system where things were exchanged, say wheat for milk. However, with the evolution of money, came the concept of *market place*. Hence, with the existence of market place, it was realized that people would be ready to pay extra if they could delivered product at the customer's door step, therefore, the concept of street vendors came into being. When the postal system came into existence, the seller started using mailer giving description of their product. Hence, it led to the concept of *mail· order cataloguing*. Then, with the development of media vehicle, came the concept of tele-shopping and the new generation of commerce is done over the internet, i.e. e-commerce.

3.1 What is E-commerce?

E-commerce refers to online transactions, that is, buying and selling of goods and services over the internet involving transaction of monetary nature. E-commerce commercial transactions are between and among organizations and individuals. E-commerce is a subset of e-business. E-business is a broader aspect comprising e-commerce, internet marketing, e- procurement etc. Transactions involving money are e-commerce activities including interaction with business partners, vendors and customers. The ability of the internet to bring together distant parts of the world in a global electronic market place and information exchange has had beneficial impact on both the developing and industrialized economies.

3.2 Evolution of E-commerce

The three stages in the evolution of e-commerce are

innovation, consolidation and reinvention. Innovation took place from 1995-2000 and was characterized by excitement and idealistic visions of markets in which quality information was equally available to both buyers and merchants. It was driven by visions of profiting from new technology, with the emphasis on quickly achieving very high market visibility. The source of financing was venture capital funds as they had their own strategy for investing. Venture capitalists (VCs) preferred to invest in large markets where there were potentially large buyers. VCs were inclined to invest in high growth businesses, as traditional retail had inherent challenges to scale quickly. The ability to acquire customers in a capital efficient way is extremely important to maintain a viable business. Hence, models that were capital efficient, quick in acquiring customers, and had large scale operations were appealing to VCs. However, so far none of the e-commerce companies in India are profit making.

However, e-commerce did not fulfil these visions during its early years and in 2000, stock market valuations collapsed for the dot.com ventures. It collapsed, as there wasn't any strong business plan for an untapped market. Investors were blindly buying new IPOs of internet companies without looking at the business model. Companies reported huge losses and hence were shut down. The stocks were highly overvalued which resulted in overly optimistic values. It all happened due to the following of the network theory i.e., the value of network increased exponentially as the series of nodes (computer hosting network) increased. The investors ignored the ability of the company to use the network to generate profits.

After 2000, e-commerce entered its second stage of development viz. the consolidation. In this stage, more traditional firms began to use the web to enhance their existing businesses and less emphasis was placed on creating new brands. In 2006, e-commerce entered its current stage, reinvention, as social networking and web 2.0 applications reinvigorated e-commerce and encouraged the development of new business models.

3.2.1 Innovation Stage and the Consolidation Stage: The major difference between the early years of e-commerce (Innovation Stage: 1995-2000), (Consolidation Stage: 2001-2006), and (Reinvention Stage: 2006 onwards) are as under:

1. During the innovation stage, e-commerce was primarily technology-driven. During the consolidation stage, it was primarily business-driven. Today's e-commerce, is still business-driven, but also audience, customer, and community-driven.
2. During the innovation stage, firms placed emphasis on revenue growth, thereby, quickly achieving a high market visibility and market share. During the consolidation stage, the emphasis was on building profitable firms. Presently, audience and social network growth are being emphasized.
3. Start-ups during the innovation stage were financed by venture capitalists, whereas those in the consolidation stage were primarily financed by traditional methods. Currently, start-ups are once again being financed by the venture capitalists, albeit with smaller investments. Also, large online firms are acquiring early stage firms.
4. During the innovation stage, e-commerce was, for the most part, ungoverned. In the consolidation stage, there was a rise in the amount of regulations and governmental controls worldwide. Presently, there is extensive government regulation and surveillance.
5. The innovation stage of e-commerce was characterized by young entrepreneurial spirit. During the consolidation stage, e-commerce was primarily dominated by the retail giants. Currently, large web-based firms are playing a major role.
6. The innovation phase was characterized by an emphasis on deconstructing traditional distribution channels and dis-intermediating existing channels. During the consolidation stage, intermediaries strengthened. Presently, there is a

proliferation of small online intermediaries that are renting out business processes of larger firms.

7. "Perfect markets" in which direct market relationships with consumers, decline of intermediaries, and lower transaction costs that occurred, resulted in intense competition and the elimination of brands, resultantly being replaced by imperfect markets. Imperfect markets are characterized by a strengthening of brand name importance, increasing information asymmetries, price discrimination, and network effects.
8. The early years of e-commerce saw an infusion of pure online businesses that thought they could achieve the first mover advantages. During the consolidation stage, successful firms used a mixed *bricks-and-clicks* strategy, combining traditional sales channels such as physical stores and printed catalogues with online efforts. Today, there is a return of pure online strategies in new markets, as well as continuing extension of the "bricks-and-clicks" strategy in traditional retail markets.
9. The early years of e-commerce were dominated by the first movers. In the consolidation stage, e-commerce was dominated by the well-endowed and experienced Fortune 500 and other traditional firms. Presently, first-mover advantages are returning in new markets as traditional web players.

The year 1995 saw the backbone of formation of e-commerce with the setting up of Amazon, Craigslist and others. In 1997, Dell was the first company to reach US$ 1 million in online sales and in 1998 Google was launched. In the second stage, which was business driven, Amazon in 2003 posted its first ever profits and Facebook was launched for the college students. The social networking sites became huge drivers of a new e-commerce wave. In the reinvention stage, which is business driven, Google acquired YouTube and surpassed US$ 21 billion in revenue. In the reinvention stage, e-commerce industry was never the same with many new companies being launched as private labels and value added services like Zalora, Tate and Tonic, as daily deal/flash deals, price comparison and social shopping sites like My Supermarket, Pinterest, as fulfilment/delivery sites like DHL, fulfilment by Amazon, and as e-commerce software platforms like Singapore Post and DHL.

In this stage, content, community and commerce converged. A striking example of this includes Tencent WeChat service. The WeChat account was an interactive account with facilities of a personal banker where China Merchant Bank allowed checking and repayment of balances including online questions via WeChat.

Similarly, it also acts as a shopping assistant and private chef. The technology and e-commerce companies have converged in reinvention phase with Apple having an Apple Store and Itunes, Google having Google Play, Google Shopping Express, Amazon having Amazon FireTV and Amazon Web Services and Alibaba having Taobao.com, Tmall.com and Alipay.com.

The early years of e-commerce can be considered a success because of the technological success that occurred, as web-enabled transactions grew from thousands to billions. The digital infrastructure proved to be a solid foundation on which to build a viable marketing channel. From a business perspective, the early years of e-commerce were a mixed success with just a tiny percentage of dot.com companies surviving.

However, the survivors have benefited from the continued growth in B2C revenues. The early years of e-commerce can also be considered a success in the sense that transfer of information has been a huge accomplishment as consumers learned to use the web to procure information about products they wanted to purchase (internet-influenced commerce).

As per the Network Readiness Index (NRI) 2021 rankings, released by the Portulans Institute on December 2, 2021, eight out of ten top positions were held by countries in Europe

(Netherlands, Sweden, Denmark, US, Finland, Switzerland, Singapore, Germany, Norway, and the United Kingdom). The top 3 positions in Asia and Pacific region for 2021 were held by Singapore, Republic of Korea and Australia. The top five countries in Asia in terms of overall ICT readiness included Singapore, Republic of Korea, Japan, China, and Malaysia. India was positioned at 67 in the lower middle-income countries group.

3.2.2 Six Principles of Networked Readiness Framework: The networked readiness framework rests on the following six principles:

1. A high-quality regulatory and business environment.
2. ICT affordability, skills, and infrastructure.
3. Role of the government, the business sector, and the population.
4. The impact of ICT on the economy and society.
5. The set of drivers, the environment, readiness, and usage—interact, co-evolve, and reinforce each other to form a virtuous cycle.
6. A networked readiness framework that should provide clear policy guidance.

Internet usage (as percentage of world total users) globally has been on the rise, with 53.4 percent in Asia, 6.7 percent in North America, 14.3 percent in Europe, 11.5 percent in Africa and 0.6 percent in Oceania, as of March 31, 2021. The main reason behind the online user growth has been the improved network infrastructure and growing need of online content consumption.

3.3 Approaches to E-commerce

There are two primary approaches to e-commerce viz. technical and behavioural. Each of these approaches is represented by several academic disciplines.

3.3.1 The Technical Side:

1. Computer scientists are interested in e-commerce as an application of internet technology.

2. Management scientists are primarily interested in building mathematical models of business processes and optimizing them to learn how businesses can exploit the internet to improve their business operations.
3. Information systems professionals are interested in e-commerce because of its implications for firm and industry value chains, industry structure, and corporate strategy.
4. Economists have focused on consumer behaviour at websites, and on the features of digital electronic markets.

3.3.2 The Behavioural Side:

1. Sociologists have focused on studies of internet usage, the role of social inequality in skewing internet benefits, and the use of the web as a personal and group communications tool.
2. Finance and accounting scholars have focused on e-commerce firm's valuation and accounting practices.
3. Management scholars have focused on entrepreneurial behaviour and the challenges faced by young firms who are required to develop organizational structures in short time spans.
4. Marketing scholars have focused on consumer response to online marketing and audiences, and position products to achieve higher returns on investment.

These approaches to e-commerce underline that what matters to customer is price, product range and browsing experience. Investors are required not to ignore the fundamental rules of investing in the stock market, such as analyzing P/E ratios, studying market trends, and reviewing business plans.

3.4 Three Broad Interrelated Themes of E-commerce

1. **Technology:** To understand e-commerce, one needs a basic understanding of the information technologies upon which it is built, including the internet and the world wide web, and a host of complimentary technologies, including personal computers, local area networks, client/server

computing, packet-switched communications, protocols such as TCP/IP, web servers, HTML, and relational databases, among others.

2. **Business:** While technology provides the infrastructure, it is the business applications—the potential for extraordinary returns on investment—that create the interest and excitement in e-commerce. New technologies present businesses and entrepreneurs with new ways of organizing production and transacting business. Therefore, one also needs to understand some key business concepts such as electronic markets, information goods, business models, firm and industry value chains, industry structure, and consumer behaviour in electronic markets.
3. **Society:** Understanding the pressures that global e-commerce place on contemporary society, is critical for the success of e-commerce marketplace. The primary societal issues include intellectual property, individual privacy, and public policy.

3.5 Features of E-commerce

There are seven features of e-commerce technology that are unique to this medium. E-commerce technology:

1. Is *ubiquitous*—it is available just about everywhere, at all times, making it possible to shop from one's desktop, at home, at work, or even from one's car.
2. Has global reach, permitting commercial transactions across cross-cultural and national boundaries, far more conveniently and cost-effectively than in traditional commerce.
3. Operates according to *universal standards* shared by all nations around the world. In contrast, most traditional commerce technologies are different in different nations.
4. Provides information *richness*, that is, the complexity and content of a message. It enables an online merchant to deliver marketing messages with text, video, and audio to millions of audience which is not possible with traditional

commerce technologies such as radio, magazines etc.

5. Is *interactive*—it allows for two-way communication between a merchant and a consumer and enables the merchant to engage a consumer in ways similar to a face-to-face experience, but on a much more massive and global scale.
6. Increases *information density* (the total amount and quality of information available to all the market participants). The internet reduces information collection, storage, processing, and communication costs while increasing the accuracy and timeliness of information. Growth in information density could result in:

- Greater price transparency: Consumers can easily find out the variety of prices in the market.
- Greater cost transparency: Consumers can discover the actual costs merchants pay for the products.
- Greater opportunities for marketers to practice price discrimination: Since marketers are able to gather much more information about their customers, they can segment the market into groups based on willingness to pay different prices for the same or nearly the same goods.

7. Permits *personalization* and *customization*—Merchants can channelize their marketing messages to specific individuals by adjusting the message to a person's name, interests, and past purchases. Because of the increase in information density, a great deal of information about the consumer's past purchases and behaviour can be stored and used by online merchants. The result is a high level of personalization and customization which is not possible with existing commerce technology.

3.6 Types of E-commerce

There are five major types of e-commerce:

1. B2C involves businesses selling to consumers and is the type of e-commerce that most consumers are likely to encounter, e.g. Taobao, Amazon.

2. B2B e-commerce involves businesses selling to other businesses and is the largest form of e-commerce, e.g., Alibaba, Snapdeal.
3. C2C is a means for consumers to sell to each other. In C2C e-commerce, the consumer prepares the product for market, places the product for auction or sale, and relies on the market maker to provide catalogue, search engine, and transaction clearing capabilities so that products can be easily displayed, discovered, and paid for, e.g., Tmall, Ebay, OLX.
4. P2P technology enables internet users to share files and computer resources directly without having to go through a central web server. Examples, Kazaa and Grokster which are music and file sharing services.
5. M-commerce involves the use of wireless digital devices, that is, mobile to enable transactions on the web.

3.7 Revenue Models of E-commerce

The five primary revenue models used by e-commerce firms are:

1. Advertising revenue model.
2. Subscription revenue model.
3. Transaction fee revenue model.
4. Sale revenue model.
5. Affiliate revenue model.

The advertising model derives its revenue by displaying paid advertisements on a website. The purpose is to convince advertisers that the site has the ability to attract a sizeable viewership, or a viewership that meets a marketing niche sought by the advertiser—practice followed by Google and Yahoo.

Revenue from CPM displays advertising on site (e.g. banners, ads and skyscrapers). CPM stands for "cost per thousand" where M denotes "Mille". The site owner such as FT.com charges advertisers a rate card price (for example ₹ 3,000 CPM) according to the number of ads shown to the site visitors.

CPC stands for "Cost per Click". Advertisers are charged not simply for the number of times their ads are displayed, but according to the number of times they are clicked. These are typically text ads similar to sponsored links within a search engine but delivered over a network of third party sites on a search engine such as the Google. Google is the innovator and offers options for different formats of ad units including text ads, display ads, streamed videos and even charges cost per action as part of its pay per action scheme.

Firms that use the subscription model offer users access to some or all of their content or services for a subscription fee—practice followed by Consumer Reports Online, Yahoo.

A range of documents can be accessed for a period of a month or a year. For example, if one has subscribed to WSJ.com for access to digital technology section for a year and Smart Insights Expert members have an annual subscription in this form. In this, payment occurs for single access to a document, video or music clip which can be downloaded. It may or may not be protected with a password or digital rights management.

Digital rights management (DRM) is the use of different technologies to protect the distribution of digital services or content such as software, music, movies, or other digital data. Firms that use the transaction fee model, derive revenue from enabling or executing transactions. For instance, transaction fees are paid to eBay when a seller is successful in auctioning of a product, and e-trade receives a transaction fee when it executes a stock transaction for a customer.

In the sales revenue model, companies draw revenue directly from the sale of goods, information, or services to consumers—as is followed by Amazon.com, LLBean.com.

In the affiliate model, sites receive referral fees or a percentage of the revenue from any sales that result from steering business to an affiliate—followed by MyPoints.com. Affiliate revenue is commission based. For example, if one displays Amazon books on its site and receives around 5 percent of the cover price as a fee from Amazon, such an arrangement is sometimes known as cost per acquisition (CPA).

3.8 Online versus Traditional Shopping

The advent of internet had an impact on human lives in all sorts of ways including the way one communicates and shops. Shopping has been done by people for the past 100 years but the way of doing has changed in the past few years. Presently, with sophistication of technology, one does not need to visit markets to do shopping. Rather, one can do it with just a click of the mouse from home over internet, and shopping from the comfort of one's home has become a part of most people's daily lives.

When retailing on the web started in 1990s, it gave rise to the debate which is still going on, that is, about online vs. traditional shopping. Even though shopping centres are still thronged by shoppers, just as they do on the internet, the question still remains, whether online shopping will conquer all or if traditional shopping will survive the increasing use of e-shopping?

3.8.1 Advantages of Online Shopping

1. Online shopping is done over internet and therefore one does not have to stand in line or go anywhere from one's home to purchase the stuff. In physical shopping, if one wants to buy, one would have to go to a nearby mall or shop and then purchase the item one likes from there.
2. In online shopping, one can quickly scroll through several stores to locate the item one wants to buy. Most of these websites are very user friendly and simple to navigate. All of this implies that the advent of online shopping has provided consumers the facility of making infinite choices in getting exactly the product they want. The demand and supply bottlenecks of the past no longer exist, hence everyone has access to everything. With shelf space not

costing much, everyone's shopping requirements can be catered to; whereas in case of physical or traditional shopping one does not have too much of choices as one has to buy the product which is available at shop and if that product is not available then either you buy the product which is your second choice or wait for that product to come and then buy. Due to limitation of shelf space, brick and mortar shops simply cannot afford to provide large varieties of products. For them, it makes economic sense to fill the limited space on their shelves with items that sell the most. These products may not necessarily be the best, but probably are the ones that are marketed the best.

3. Online shopping is transparent in the sense that one can compare the price of product over different websites to ensure that he or she buys the product at cheapest price. However, in case of physical shopping one does not have this luxury because the buyer has to purchase the product at a price which is quoted by seller as there is no way of finding whether the price quoted by the seller is fair or not.
4. In case of online shopping, thousands of different products are available at one place or website whereas in case of physical shopping this is not possible and hence if one wants to buy a mobile and trousers then one would have to go to different shops as these products are different and hence leads to wastage of time. Hence, one can say that when it comes to saving time, online shopping definitely scores over physical shopping.

3.8.2 Disadvantages of Online Shopping

1. Seeing and touching a product is also an important factor for many people when they buy things. For example, most people would not buy a piece of expensive jewellery only on the basis of a picture on a website. Consumers may carry out research online for high priced items like properties and cars, but want to see the piece of real estate or visit a car showroom and test drive a car before

finalising a deal. Therefore, chances are slim for the internet to capture a share of the market of industries which are more suitable for traditional shopping.

2. In online shopping if one is buying products like shoes or clothes then one cannot try the product before placing the order and therefore the chances of actual product being different from the perceived product is high. Whereas, in case of traditional shopping, there is no such risk because a consumer tries it first and then buys and therefore there is no scope of difference between the actual and the perceived product.
3. Traditional shopping makes sure that one could get the product immediately the moment money is paid. This is very useful in the case of urgent need daily necessities like shampoo, tissues etc. If one may need an item right now, for instance, grocery items, buying it from a retail store is the only option.
4. Online shopping is used by people who are tech savvy and therefore it is mostly used by young people. However, in recent times, middle age and older age people too are getting used to it. On the contrary, physical shopping is done by old people or by those who are not that familiar with the technological advancements in e-commerce and its benefits and consider online shopping risky because of the fear of fraud.
5. A traditional retailer bestows personalised human contact, which is not available on the internet. Besides, for many people, shopping is a source of entertainment, almost a social rite.

But the rising popularity of shopping online shows that for an increasing number of people factors like inconvenience, crowd, going all the way to the shop only to find the product they are looking for being out of stock, outweigh the few advantages that traditional shopping has to offer.

4

Factors Affecting Growth of E-commerce

There are many factors that may influence the rate of growth of e-commerce.

4.1 Trust in the Medium

The most significant constraint is the degree to which suppliers and customers are familiar with and can trust the medium, especially for making payments. Customers may trust purchasing online only if transactions are fast, convenient and secure.

Trust can be an important factor in business to consumer (B2C) e-commerce. It gives consumers faith to buy products or services even if an e-trader is unknown. It encourages greater use of e-commerce technologies, makes the e-transaction process easier, and enhances the level of acceptance. It leads to improvement in consumer commitment, raises customer satisfaction, introduces the concept of loyalty, sustains long-term relationships with customers and helps in acquiring competitive benefit and may motivate purchases.

Trust is a complicated concept and has multiple sides which need to be addressed. There are a number of researchers who have continuously approached the 'trust' issue from a technical side such as internet and network security and even web interface design. However, according to Klang (2001) and Ratnasingham and Kumar (2000), considering just the technical perceptions will not guarantee trust in e-commerce.

Major research has outlined the influence of usefulness towards the usage of e-commerce. The real reason why customers would use e-commerce is that they find it a useful facility for conducting shopping online.

4.2 Degree of Awareness

Furthermore, according to Sathye's (1999) research, the use of online banking services is new knowledge to many customers, and the lack of awareness of online banking is a crucial factor in preventing customers from adopting it. In his study of 500 Australian customers, he concluded that customers were not aware of the potential benefits of online banking. This was supported by another study by Howcroft et al., (2002) in which they found that the issue of lack of awareness and knowledge of online banking services is a hindrance to adopt e-commerce. Suki and Ramayah (2010) studied user acceptance of the e-Government services in Malaysia. Their results indicate that the important determinants of user acceptance of the e-Government services are perceived usefulness, ease of use, compatibility, interpersonal influence, external influence, self-efficacy, facilitating conditions, attitude, subjective norms, perceived behavioural control, and intention to use e-Government services/system (Source: Kabango,2015).

The concerns about the working, risks and benefits of electronic commerce can be made clear through public awareness programmes. WITSA countries (Canada, Czech Republic, England, Germany, Israel, Japan, Netherlands, South Africa, Sweden, Brazil, Lithuania, New Zealand, Sweden, Thailand and the US) reported a reasonably high awareness in their markets of electronic commerce (Source: The World Information Technology and Services Alliance, International Survey of Electronic Commerce, 2000).

4.3 Skill Gap

Skill gap is a major hindrance for the development of electronic commerce markets. There is need for people to learn complicated operating systems, and also learn a set of sophisticated skills to make effective use of the internet and e-commerce capabilities. US, Germany and UK had relaxed visa rules to encourage workers with internet skills to emigrate to their countries. India's abundant skilled and English speaking manpower rates high in areas such as qualifications, capabilities, quality of work, and work ethics and it turned out to be a 'brain-gain' for the Western and capitalist economies. Indian professionals adapted and succeeded quickly in the new environment. There are several success stories of Indian expatriates in the Silicon Valley, where persons of Indian origin run about 30 percent of the existing software and e-commerce companies.

4.4 Public Policy

Electronic commerce has to deal with issues on public policy, such as taxation, regulation, security and privacy. The development of electronic commerce has changed the way international business is conducted and requires a review of tax policies and laws, meant for traditional commerce.

WITSA members identified local or state taxes and foreign taxes such as value added tax as most harmful to the viability of electronic commerce businesses in their country.

Electronic commerce should compete with traditional commerce on a level playing field. A global perspective is required when addressing this issue, as electronic commerce cuts across national boundaries.

OECD is the only trans-national body tackling the issue of consumer protection in electronic commerce through self-regulation. In an effort to facilitate trans-border electronic commerce, the Consumer Policy Division of OECD is drawing up guidelines for its member countries. It addresses issues such as jurisdiction, collection of personal information and how complaints can be handled.

4.5 Costs Involved and Technology Limitations

Electronic commerce requires substantial investment such as investment in call centres, warehouses and office buildings. The costs involved in updating business processes and encouraging new corporate cultures are high.

Speed, internet penetration, last mile connectivity and the usability of electronic commerce systems, i.e., lack of local content are the most common technology issues. Technological concerns are not as important as the issues of trust, familiarity and understanding.

Also, the online shopping experience will not be able to replace social and cultural experience that many seek from the traditional shopping environment. Hence, social and cultural limitations will be tougher to overcome than technological limitations.

4.6 Growth of E-commerce in Various Countries

1. **China:** At present China is the biggest e-commerce market in the world. The growth of e-commerce in China has surpassed the combined e-commerce growth of the US and Europe in 2019. The forecast is that Chinese e-commerce market will reach over US $ 3 trillion in 2024. The internet users are growing with an estimation of 710 million internet users.
2. **US:** It is at number two to China and projections are that by 2025 online retail sales will hit US$ 563.4 billion.
3. **UK:** The biggest e-commerce websites in UK include AmazonUK, Argos and Play.com. It is forecasted that by 2025, e-commerce sales in the country would reach more than US $ 119 billion.
4. **Japan:** E-commerce sales are led by Rakuten, the largest online retailer in Japan. It also provides services in other areas such as banking services that include loans and mortgages, travel websites, brokerage services for securities and even managing professional sports teams. The e-commerce market in Japan if forecasted to reach US$ 3.40 billion by 2025.
5. **Germany:** It is one of the major e-commerce markets and after Brexit it became the top country in the EU. The estimation is that its annual B2C online sales will be almost $85 bn. The major players are ebay and Germany's local online retailer Otto.

6. **France:** E-commerce market is led by Odigeo, the largest travel company in France and Cdiscount. Amazon is also prevalent in France, but it did not report its French sales numbers publicly. The revenue from e-commerce is expected to grow to over US$ 72 billion in 2025.
7. **South Korea:** It is one of the first countries to launch commercial 5G network services. Its revenue from e-commerce is expected to reach US$ 99.2 billion by 2025. It is leading m-commerce markets and major players include Gmarket and Coupang.
8. **Canada:** Amazon has a strong position in the Canadian e-commerce market netting a sale of US$ 9.8 billion in 2021. Online sites Walmart and Costco were positioned at number 2 and 3 respectively. E-commerce revenues in Canada are projected to surpass US$ 40 billion by 2024.
9. **Russia:** E-commerce revenue in the country is projected at US$ 31.8 billion by 2025. It is the largest online market in Europe. Ulmart, Citilink and Ozon are the biggest online retailers.
10. **Brazil:** B2W is the largest online retailer not only in Brazil, but in Latin America as well. It has acquired multiple logistics companies in Brazil that specializes in delivery of products in order to increase the efficiency and overall delivery capabilities in more areas of the country. The revenue from e-commerce sales is forecasted to be 31.5 bn US $ by 2025. The revenue more than doubled in 2020.

4.7 Comparison of China and US

The above suggests that China is at the top of the list and US is at number two, which makes for an interesting comparison of the two giants of world economy. In 2021, China contributed to more than half of the world's e-commerce retail sales, with the sales value surpassing the combined total of Europe and the United States.

US e-retail sales were double that of China in 2010, but in 2013 and 2014, China had overtaken the US to become the world's largest national e-commerce market.

China was leading the number of internet users at 904,000,000 and its internet penetration was 62.8 percent (as of June 2020). In US, number of internet users was pegged at 313,322,868 and internet penetration was 89.8 percent (as of June 2020). Therefore, the growth in internet users from 2000-2021 was 3796 percent in China and 328 percent in US.

With the increased use of smart phones in China, even small online platforms were able to gain market share as 83.4 percent of internet users had used mobile phones to access internet (June 2014). The increased mobile data use represents how e-commerce had been growing in China. Also, the fixed broadband subscribers had increased much faster than those in US as in China. It had increased almost three times, from 66 million in 2007 to 189 million in 2013 whereas in US, it increased from 70 million in 2007 to 94 million in 2013, with 69.6 percent internet users in China using desktop to access internet (June 2014) (Source: CKGSB).

Chinese internet surfers preferred to use their native language to search for information that may say for the success of Alibaba in China as it had focussed on local variables, be it language, payment methods, local shopping habits or taste. Chinese consumers had historically preferred to pay by cash on delivery (COD) unlike US, where e-commerce was dependent on credit card system. Moreover, internet users for the year 2014 in China were much younger than those in US as it was 31 percent in age group 20-29 and 5 percent in age group 50-59. Comparatively, in US, it was 18 age group in 25-34 and 26 age group in 55+ age group (Source: CKGSB).

The rise in e-commerce sales in China may be attributed to the Chinese companies' characteristics of inclusion, efficiency and innovation.

The dynamic growth and rapid spread of e-commerce in China can best be illustrated by the Shaji phenomenon. The economy of Dongfeng village in Shaji town (Jiangsu Province) shifted from pig farming in the 1980s to plastic waste recycling in the 1990s. In 2006, a migrant from the village returned to open an online shop, to sell simple furniture. His success encouraged other villagers to do likewise, and by the end of 2010, the village had 6 board processing factories, 2 metal parts factories, 15 logistics and shipping companies, and 7 computer stores serving 400 households engaged in online sales throughout China and even in neighbouring countries. Shaji was one of the first "Taobao villages" named after an online shopping platform run by the Alibaba Group where at least 10 percent of the households were engaged in online commerce. The Taobao villages and the rise of e-commerce in China illustrate how internet promotes inclusion, efficiency, and innovation.

While the economies of China's coastal urban areas have grown rapidly over the last three decades, rural and western parts of the country have lagged behind. But China's large investments in rural connectivity had begun to pay off. Online commerce has allowed producers in towns and villages to participate in the national and even global economy. At the end of 2014, there were more than 70,000 merchants in 200 Taobao villages, and many more in other rural areas. Most of the stores are small, with an average of 2.5 employees. About one-third of owners are female, and one-fifth was previously unemployed. One of Alibaba's top entpreneurs confined to a wheelchair after an accident, built a thriving online livestock business.

Besides the Taobao e-commerce site for consumers, Alibaba and other Chinese firms operate business-to-business platforms. They facilitate intra- and inter-industry trade in China's production sector, as well as exports. They also make it easier for the foreign firms to sell in China. Consumers benefit from greater selection and convenience on online retail sites. Online trade has not only helped raise rural incomes but also made shopping more efficient. Purchasing power in rural areas was only about one-third than in the cities, but the aggregate consumption of China's 650 million rural residents is vast, contributing to the national goal of moving from an export and investment driven economy to more consumption based economy. The boom in online trade has spawned numerous logistics companies that provide quick delivery, sometimes by bicycle in towns and villages.

Taobao and other e-commerce platforms are examples of innovation generated by the economies of scale that emerge when transaction costs drop drastically. Since these platforms are highly automated, fees can be kept low, and operations are often financed by advertising alone. However, the issue of creating trust in the market and preventing fraud are addressed by online ratings, escrow services, and conflict resolution mechanisms.

One of the most valuable assets Alibaba and other e-commerce operators accumulate is data. Each transaction contributes to better knowledge about the economy and consumer behaviour. This information supports new business lines, such as extending credit to small firms based on automated evaluations of creditworthiness. This can also advance financial inclusion. In early 2015, for instance, Alibaba's Ant Financial teamed up with the International Finance Corporation to expand credit to female entrepreneurs in China.

It is also attributed to Chinese companies' vision of tailoring its country websites to national culture such as tailored communication, ease of understanding, intuitive operations, and trust. These aspects had enhanced the customer's experience and intention to reuse the site.

5

Issues in E-commerce

Internet and e-commerce have led to certain issues for domestic economy, such as, accessibility, expense, education or e-literacy, security, market access, and characterization. How to ensure access at reasonable cost? How to tackle the growing digital divide? What technologies are required and what standards are to be set? How to monitor and how to tax? India not only has to find solutions to the above questions but also the means and resources to implement the policies.

5.1 Financial Issues

5.1.1 Customs and Taxation: Internet does not have fixed boundaries which had been there for physical trade of goods. Therefore, it is possible to tax products ordered over the internet but delivered physically. However, it is difficult to tax when the product or service is delivered electronically. Since, countries all over the world need revenue they may therefore impose tax on global electronic commerce.

The existing taxation rules of permanent establishment are difficult to apply as there is no physical location of these transactions, hence rendering revenue jurisdiction difficult. Also, e-commerce had changed the pattern of intermediation by banks and other institutions, thereby limiting the ability of authorities to collect withholding tax.

Taxes are either source-based or destination-based. Further, applying source based taxes to e-commerce would have compliance and administrative cost advantages over destination-based tax; but still the problem of tax evasion would remain. Hence, tax administration has to maximise the potential "efficiency gains" out of technology and also to protect the revenue base.

In India, no effort had been made to prepare clear cut taxation policy for e-commerce transactions. WTO had decided not to tax e-commerce transaction till 2017. Further, countries such as US are in favour of tax-less internet economy, but countries such as India, China etc. are in favour of tariff on electronic commerce. These countries argued that, US has an unfair share of revenue since most of the internet traffic is routed through the US.

5.1.2 Electronic Payment Systems: With new technology, one can make payment for goods and services over the internet. Various methods such as credit and debit card networks link electronic banking and payment systems with new retail market through internet.

Vasudevan Committee on the Technological Upgradation of the Banking Sector recommended that "the RBI may promote amendment to the RBI Act, 1934, and assume the regulatory and supervisory powers on payment and settlement systems. Simultaneously, the RBI may promote a new legislation on electronic funds transfer (EFT), to facilitate multiple payment systems, to be set up for banks and financial institutions.

In the Reserve Bank of India Act, 1934, Chapter-III D of the IT Act, 1999 had to be included after Chapter IIIC, to deal with electronic funds transfer systems. However, under Section 58 of the Reserve Bank of India Act, 1934, notification for Regulation for Electronic Funds Transfer System is done.

The Reserve Bank of India on August 19, 2015, granted 'in-principle' approval to 11 entities, viz. Reliance Industries, Aditya Birla Nuvo, Paytm, Vodafone, and Airtel etc., to set up payment banks in the country. The 'in-principle' approval granted was valid for a period of 18 months, during which the said entities had to comply with the requirements under the guidelines and fulfil the other conditions as may be stipulated by the Reserve Bank of India.

Payment gateways for e-commerce transactions are one of the most essential requirements for establishing and developing e-commerce. These need to be well established and strengthened in India.

5.2 Legal Issues

5.2.1 Uniform Commercial Code: For the growth of electronic commerce, it is necessary that the governments frame domestic and global uniform commercial legal framework which recognizes, facilitates, and enforces electronic transactions worldwide.

The growth of global electronic commerce depends upon the buyers and sellers degree of certainty to the exposure to liability for any damage that may occur from their actions. Inconsistent local laws and uncertainty regarding jurisdiction, would increase litigation and hence unnecessary costs will be created to be borne by the consumers. Therefore, it is necessary that all the nations work with each other to clarify jurisdictional rules and enforce contract provisions between buyers and sellers.

Therefore, the development of global electronic commerce will provide an opportunity to take advantage of new technology, thereby, creating legal rule and streamlining the functions done manually.

In the context of India, the laws require change. The law against computer crimes and other cyber laws should be introduced so that the information infrastructure of the countries be built. The laws may be framed for Electronic Data Interchange (EDI), Electronic Commerce, Electronic Funds Transfer, Electronic Cash, Copyright and Digital Intellectual Property rights etc. For example a change in Evidence Act to recognize digital signatures, changes in Evidence Act, 1872, Indian Penal Code, 1860 and Indian Patents Act General Clauses/Act should be considered to recognise the emergence of technology, keeping in view the following:

1. Prevention of computer crimes.
2. Digital signatures especially related to electronic funds transfer.

3. Copyright and digital intellectual property rights especially with regard to internet and world wide web.
4. Electronic governance.
5. Computerization of land records.
6. Bar coding of all consumer goods and related amendments in the Weights and Measures Act.
7. Cryptography and encryption.
8. Privacy of data.

The IT Act, 1999 seeks to address some of these issues, especially relating to cyber crimes and digital signatures, but several issues are still left unaddressed.

India is supposed to be a software superpower but the activity of e-commerce has started very late, hence, India needs to comprehend the laws, and national debates may be initiated so that India can put forward its views regarding laws to be prepared at WTO and fetch a favourable response.

5.2.2 Intellectual Property Protection: There will be sale and licensing of intellectual property due to commerce on the internet. For the growth of e-commerce, sellers have to be sure that intellectual property will not be stolen and buyers had to be sure that they are buying authentic product. Therefore, international agreement for clear and effective copyright, patent, and trademark protection are required to prevent piracy and fraud. Encryption may help in preventing piracy but effective legal framework is also necessary to deter fraud and theft of intellectual property and to provide effective legal recourse when these crimes occur. Further, increased public education about intellectual property in the information age will also contribute to the successful implementation and growth of the Global Information Infrastructure.

In India, the IPR Cell in MIT (earlier DoE) is a facilitator for creation, ownership and protection of IPR in electronics and information technology. The IPR Cell had initiated a project on development of Electronic Copyright Management System for Indian environment and for this market oriented consensus based approach is being followed so that the developed technology meets the requirements.

5.2.3 Privacy: Issue of privacy is also major concern and had been raised in many countries around the world. Many countries had enacted laws, implemented industry self-regulation and had instituted administrative solutions designed to safeguard their citizens' privacy. The different countries will adopt different policies which might disrupt trans-border data flows. Therefore, it is necessary that various countries should discuss and try to build support for industry-developed solutions to privacy problems and flow of data on the internet is not affected.

The GII (Global Information Infrastructure) facilitates the collection, re-use, and instantaneous transmissions of information, but it has to be managed with care so that privacy and free flow of information is balanced. In India, it is in the development stage as few organizations particularly, defence sector are involved exclusively for the development of cryptography techniques, protocols and the products to enable privacy and security. IDRBT is also working on solutions required by the banking and financial sector of the country.

Since, Department of Telecommunications does not allow the encrypted signal on their network that is why extensive development in this area had not taken place. Secondly, worldwide, the cryptographic products are licensed items and the license to the country is not easily available for products of key length of more than 56 bits. Indian industry mainly assembles PCs and so the cryptographic product has been limited to the PC market. Further, higher end systems are not produced in the country, so the progress of the work is slow, since know-how of the system is not available.

5.3 Market Access Issues

5.3.1 Telecommunications Infrastructure and IT: The growth of electronic commerce depends upon a modern, seamless, telecommunications network and the computers and information appliances that connect to it. But in India, telecommunications policies are hindering the development of advanced digital networks as telecommunications services often are too expensive, bandwidth is limited, and services for mission and time critical applications are unavailable or unreliable.

The numerous constraints in the network may impede the evolution of services requiring higher bandwidth. It should be ensured that online service providers reach end-users on reasonable and non discriminatory terms and conditions. If there exist genuine market, then only it will lead to increased competition, improved telecommunications infrastructures, more customer choice, lower prices and increased and improved services.

The main issue is the relative complexity of getting on, and using, the Internet acts as a deterrent to many consumers. For consumer the "ease of buying" is the underestimated factor in its purchasing decision. Presently, the buying interface over the internet is discouraging to most consumers. The interface metrics of a TV style device (turn it on and change channels) are easier to use as compared to existing computers.

Further, the important aspect of interface is how goods and services offered for sale is being represented (visual as well as auditory) on the internet. Since, online shopping has advantages for sellers such as reduced transport and storage cost, the benefits for buyers may vary, as those in cities may have benefit but for those in rural areas, the benefits are less.

Bandwidth is defined as the carrying capacity of a network, or how much data can be transferred in a given time. The importance of bandwidth is that it determines the extent to which internet *delivery* of digital products is feasible. Immediate delivery via the internet may be more attractive to consumers than deferred delivery via the ordinary mail system. In addition, certain kinds of entertainment, which appeal to consumers, rely on higher bandwidth.

Infrastructure issues to be considered for bandwidth are:

1. Leased lines,

2. Local loops pricing,
3. Interconnection,
4. Attaching equipment to the network, and
5. Multimedia over internet.

Also, countries have different levels of telecom infrastructure, which may be an obstacle to the global provision and use of some internet-based services.

India has also recognized this agent of technological change as a key source of industrial competitiveness and economic growth. It has realized that in times to come, progress in information technology would have the greatest influence on the global economy, making it possible to collect, process and transmit information at lightning speed at lesser cost, thereby increasing productivity, returns on capital, quality and efficiency in all sectors of the economy.

However, there is a problem of last mile connectivity. As one steps out of Delhi or any other metro, one would witness the network being converted from 3G/4G to basic network. Therefore, the focus should be on development of infrastructure, manpower development, education, software exports, employment, low-cost computers, chip manufacturing, internet proliferation and new laws.

The liberalization of government procedures and policies had attracted a large number of companies from overseas as well as India to set up operations, but growth and development of infrastructure has not kept pace with the growth of the industry in India. Hence, the focus should be on:

1. Physical designing of IT infrastructure.
2. Institutional framework.
3. Internet proliferation and development of India as a major internet hub.
4. Human resource development.
5. Hardware development.

In order to understand the commercial and cultural potential of internet, consumers may have confidence that the goods and services offered are not counterfeit and will get the value for money, that is, will get what they pay for and if not, recourse or redress will be available.

Further, it is important to develop internet content in the country, that is, to bring internet traffic to Indian websites which focuses on Indian culture, heritage etc. Therefore, a policy initiation is required for the proliferation of internet and development of Indian content on the internet and at the same time to ensure adequate regulation on the type of content.

5.3.2 Technical Standards: For the growth of e-commerce, standards are important as it allows products and services from different vendors to work together, but also encourage competition and reduce uncertainty in the global marketplace. Premature standardization, however, can "lock in" outdated technology. Standards can also be employed as non-tariff trade barriers, to *lock out* non-indigenous businesses from a particular national market.

To ensure the growth of global electronic commerce over the internet, standards will be needed to assure reliability, interoperability, ease of use and scalability in areas such as:

1. Electronic payments;
2. Security (confidentiality, authentication, data integrity, access control, non- repudiation);
3. Security services infrastructure (e.g. public key certificate authorities);
4. Electronic copyright management systems;
5. Video and tele-conferencing;
6. High-speed network technologies.
7. Digital object and data interchange.

Countries such as US and EU had created standards for e-commerce, whereas India has yet to develop its own standard, in line with the business models.

5.3.3 Security: For wider use of internet for e-commerce, it is important that internet users have confidence that their communications and data are safe from unauthorized access or modification. Therefore, the requirements are as under:

1. Secure and reliable telecommunications networks.

2. Effective means for protecting the information systems attached to those networks.
3. Effective means for authenticating and ensuring confidentiality of electronic information to protect data from unauthorized use.
4. Users who understand how to protect their systems and their data.

To achieve these goals, it is necessary to have a spectrum of technologies such as encryption, authentication, password controls, firewalls, etc. and for effective use of these technologies, there should be trustworthy key and security management infrastructure.

In India, a start had been made regards the use of electronic commerce (EC) and electronic data interchange (EDI) by numerous agencies in the country. The EC and EDI involves communication of information related to trade and finance and would result in transaction between private and public sector, in both domestic and international communities. The success and growth of EC and EDI, however, would depend upon how the issues concerning legal (such as tampering with data, message etc.), security and performance of hardware, software and communication etc. are resolved.

5.4 Characterization Issues

As technologies converge and content becomes increasingly more portable, the boundaries between "goods" and "services" blur as well as the distinguishing characteristics that have historically separated software, telecommunications services, computer services, and audio-visual services (e.g., multimedia online games). It is within this environment of fast-paced technological change and the resulting uncertainty of what/how WTO rules apply to digital products that WTO members must prepare to make decisions regarding the application of the rules-based trading system to digital products. "Digital products" include software, movies, music, books-on-tape, and games that can be traded on a physical carrier medium such as a disc, VHS tape, CD, or book or electronically via the internet.

The WTO Report, 1998, raised the possibility that in principle, the "digits" traded on internet could be viewed as goods, services or even something else. Which of these characterizations is chosen determines whether this trade is subject to the rules laid down under the General Agreement on Tariffs and Trade (GATT), General Agreement on Trade in Services (GATS), or a combination of these two or an entirely new agreement.

There is no ambiguity at present regarding the status of the goods ordered and paid for on internet but delivered physically in a conventional manner. Except for the order and payment themselves, these transactions are treated as goods trade and the GATT discipline applies to them. But, the ambiguity arises only when the goods are delivered on the internet.

Actually, any deliveries made by internet would seem to resemble services. However, there are products delivered by internet that have counterparts in physical and merchandise trade. The examples are books, videos, music CDs and computer software. When imported in physical form, these products are treated as goods with the GATT discipline. But can they be treated as services when delivered by internet? Or, in conformity with their physical counterparts, should they be treated as goods?

One extreme possibility is to characterize all transmissions on internet as goods, with GATT discipline applied to them. Such a characterization accompanied by a ban on custom duties on the transmissions, currently in place, would amount to WTO members committing themselves to complete free trade in all transactions routed by internet. This is because national treatment and MFN status are general obligations under GATT. By accepting the GATT discipline, under national treatment, the member countries would give up their right to discriminate against internet imports as far as domestic taxes are concerned. Also, the ban on customs duty would bind their tariffs on internet imports at zero.

The member countries made their commitments in the Uruguay round (UR) and post-UR negotiations on services based on the assumption that most of those transactions were services rather than goods.

At the other extreme, both GATT and GATS can be abandoned and an entirely new discipline can be developed for internet trade. However, a search for a new discipline for e-commerce makes little sense. Internet services, which include internet service providers and phone lines on which transmissions flow, are already subject to GATS and the Agreement on Basic Telecommunications. All electronic transmissions that flow on internet, on the other hand, have counterparts in either goods trade or services trade. As such, the rules necessary to regulate that trade can be found in GATT or GATS.

Thus, the real choice is between applying GATS to all the internet trade, or GATT to that trade for which physical counterparts also exist, and GATS to all other e-trade. At one level, it may be argued that at the time internet transmissions cross the border between the two countries, they do not have a physically traded counterpart. The eventual transformation of the transmission into a good such as a book or CD does not negate the fact that at the border, the transmission did not have a physically traded counterpart. Indeed, in many cases, the transmission may not be turned into the physically traded counterpart at all. For example, the recipient may continue to store it in the digital form with books read on the screen and music played directly on the computer.

Under a mixed definition, in any trade dispute involving internet trade, panels will have to first decide whether the object of dispute is a good or a service to determine whether the rules of GATT or GATS have to be applied while evaluating the dispute.

Across the board definition, nevertheless, raises some efficiency issues that must be addressed. Thus, consider the issue of tariffs, which are applicable to products imported in physical form but not when transmitted electronically. As long as the cost of electronic transmission is lower than that of physical delivery, the presence of tariffs on the latter poses no problem. Effectively, the electronic transmission offers the product to the country at a price lower than that available through physical delivery.

However, for developing countries, this is an unlikely scenario. In these countries, most consumers do not have computers or internet access. A likely scenario, therefore, is one in which a handful of independent entrepreneurs will receive the product by internet, convert it into physical form such as CDs and sell the latter to consumers. But this activity may itself be costly, using up real resources.

6

Growth of Service Sector and E-commerce in India

6.1 Growth of Services Sector in India

It is well-known that as an economy develops, the shares of industrial and service sectors in GDP increase at the cost of the agricultural sector. The compositional shift in favour of the services sector, brought about by the rapid expansion of the service sector, is in line with the development experience of a number of countries.

The services sector has been the key driver of growth of the Indian economy in recent years. Although the growth of the Indian services sector has been broad-based, certain infrastructure services such as communications and insurance and banking have grown more rapidly, underpinning growth of the services sector as a whole. India has emerged as one of the leading exporters of commercial services in the world.

The structure of the economy has also undergone significant changes over time. Between 1950-51 and 1980-81, the industrial sector registered a higher growth rate than the services sector. The converse has been the case since then. The share of the services sector started growing rapidly thereafter and this phenomenon became more pronounced in the 1990s. The entire decline in share of agriculture has been balanced by an increase in share of the services sector. Thus, the resilience of the economy to shocks owe to the services sector which has the largest share and most consistent growth performance.

India has witnessed a services-dominated pattern of growth in gross domestic product (GDP) since the early 1990s. The sectoral shift in favour of services sector over the last two decades has taken place in the face of an almost stagnant share of industry and a reduced share of agriculture in GDP. As a matter of fact, it is the growth performance of the services sector which is sustaining the overall growth of the Indian economy in the face of a stagnating agricultural sector.

The remarkable performance of the services sector is attributable to a host of factors—internal and external—the following being the leading ones:

1. Liberalization of the financial sector.
2. Industrial sector reforms.
3. Reforms in infrastructure services.
4. External demand, the typical example of which is the software industry.

Besides deregulation and globalization, a number of qualitative factors that have resulted in the growth of services include increasing affluence, career consciousness, more leisure time, increasing complexity of life and greater life expectancy.

The commercial market for services is huge and is virtually growing all over the world. In middle and low-income economies, the service sector accounts for the largest share of total economic output. The impetus that services have given to India's growth has been equally impressive.

The market for services, therefore, has become more competitive and has shifted its focus from internal performance such as production to external interests such as satisfaction and customers' perception of service quality. With basic offers gaining parity, quality service has become the key source of differentiation.

6.1.1 Physical Infrastructure: The quality of physical infrastructure and infrastructural services is crucial for the competitiveness of the services sector, although the inter se importance of individual elements of infrastructure differs from sub-sector to sub-sector. Telecommunications, power, roads, railways, ports, airports are all important for the efficiency of the services sector. The telecommunications sector in India stands apart as it can be said to have reached world standards. However, there are serious shortcomings in all other areas resulting in high logistics cost for service enterprises.

The power situation in the country has remained bad with deficiencies in both quality and quantity of electricity supplies. Supplies have been increasing but they have been outstripped by demand with the result that shortfall between peak demand and availability has increased in the past few years.

The most important physical infrastructure needs of IT and BPO are power and telecommunications, but there is significant dependence on urban infrastructure including road transport as well. The personnel need to move speedily from their homes to workplace and they require good urban infrastructure for providing them with quality of life. Proximity to airports and good international air connections are also critical to enable them to travel frequently to foreign destinations. With all these facilities the industry requires office space.

Developments following the end of Government of India monopoly in public telecommunications resulting in large capacity creation by the private sector and significant decline in tariffs coupled with improvement in service quality have been one of the factors contributing to the growth of IT and BPO.

On the air transport front, huge improvements have already taken place in international connectivity due to the adoption virtually of Open Skies Policy and domestic deregulation has led to the growth of private domestic airlines, which have not only increased the frequency of connections domestically but also resulted in reduction of fares. Problems remain in airport infrastructure due to congestion arising from rapid growth of traffic, but these are receiving due attention.

6.2 Taxation of Services in India

Till 1994, Indian tax system traditionally relied on commodity taxation for generating revenue for the Central and State Governments. The two major commodity taxes of the Central Government were excise duties and customs duties while at the level of the States, sales tax/VAT was the main commodity tax. Tax revenue from the agricultural sector being negligible, the industrial sector continued to constitute the only principal tax base till the mid-1990s. The extension of excise duties to more and more commodities of the industrial/manufacturing sector reached a saturation point in due course of time.

The composition of national income in India had changed steadily over the years. While the share of agriculture and allied activities in the gross domestic product (GDP) had declined, that of the tertiary sector had increased. The expansion of services sector was conducive for employment generation and improved quality of life. The compositional shift of GDP in favour of the services sector was in line with the development experience of a number of countries. It is well-known that as an economy develops, the shares of industrial and service sectors in GDP increase at the cost of the agricultural sector.

Despite the fact that the services sector had shown substantial buoyancy, it remained outside the tax net till 1994. This pattern of tax structure development in India was contrary to the experience of most other countries where taxation of commodities and services grew hand in hand. In this connection, the Finance Minister, in his 1994-95 Budget Speech to Parliament, observed, "There is no sound reason for exempting services from taxation when goods are taxed and many countries treat goods and services alike for tax purpose". [1]

Tax Reforms Committee (TRC) [Chairman: Raja Chelliah], 1991 also recommended imposition of tax on certain select services, viz. advertising, non-life insurance and telephone services and services of stock brokers.

Thus, in order to impart buoyancy to government revenues and to provide consistency and equity in the tax structure via-a-via the composition of income, a modest effort was made in the 1994-95 budget when a 5 percent tax was imposed on telephone and non-life insurance services and services of stock brokers with effect from July 1, 1994.

The introduction of service tax ushered in a major structural change in the system of indirect taxes in the form of a wider tax base and facilitated the process of rationalization of excise duties, resulting in lower tax burden on productive sectors. Over the years, the number of services subject to service tax increased and so also the rate leviable on them.

The expanding base of service tax provided a promising source of revenue, but there were some caveats which had to be kept in mind. First, the scope for expanding the service tax net to more and more services got narrower as the net was widened. The contribution of the expanding net, therefore, reduced over time. Second, the preponderance of small service providers below the taxable limit of turnover constrained the scope of revenue mobilization beyond a certain level.

The introduction of the service tax was a mixed blessing. While it broadened the tax base, its structure was complex. The tax was levied on specified services, classified into one hundred odd different categories. This approach spawned many disputes about the scope of each category. Unlike goods, services are malleable, and can and are often packaged into composite bundles that include taxable as well as non-taxable elements. Also, there is no standardized nomenclature for services, such as the Harmonised System Nomenclature (HSN) for goods.

Furthermore, there was a complicated rate structure. Although there was one statutory rate, in practice there were 10 other rates because of the so-called *abatement* which amounted to fixing a rate different from the standard rate and not allowing further input tax credits. Abatement was necessitated, in some part, because of uncertainty in the base, and specifically being unable to distinguish *goods* from *services*. Further, there was incomplete provision of input tax crediting for goods, and incomplete cross-crediting between goods and services. Added to this was the Central sales tax (CST) which was levied on the sale or purchase of goods in the course of inter-State trade.

The key problem with the service tax was the basic approach of levying it on specified services, each of which generated an extensive debate as to what was included in the base. Ideally, the tax base should be defined to include all services, with a limited list of exclusions (the so-called negative list). The Government was reluctant to adopt this approach for the fear that it could bring into the tax net many services that are politically sensitive.

Service tax was abolished by Section 17 of Constitution (One Hundred and First Amendment) Act, 2016 to pave way for the introduction of GST.

6.3 Growth of E-commerce in India

Globalisation and the new 'digital economy' are creating a major impact on the world economy. Markets, of every country have been affected by changes in the global economic environment, and will continue to affect business and people. E-commerce has a significant impact on the services sector as this is not only the fastest growing sector but also the sector with the greatest potential for offering digitised service and transactions.

E-commerce affects the economic relations between and within countries and companies. A country like, India not only needs to address its potential for the growth of trade and industry but also as a means of survival in the new world of e-commerce based trade and business. As discussed earlier and based on international experience, expansion will depend on several factors such physical infrastructure, that is, the telecommunication network, financial and legal framework, that is, business and trade environment conducive to e-commerce, availability and price of hardware (computers, routers, switches, etc.) and software and human resource and education standards and policies of the country.

India's position in the digital world is due to its software exports and its software professionals (who are often part of the service export). There has been a shift in the Indian IT world from software towards electronic commerce.

6.3.1 Areas of E-commerce: E- commerce encompasses three areas:

1. Software exports (body shopping to e-commerce services).
2. Web-enabled services (transcription services to call centres).
3. E-business and e-trade (dot.coms, portals, services, and old and new economyglobal supply chains).

In the first area, there is a shift from low-end software solutions (business process outsource) to definitive sectoral software projects (such as application software, databases etc.) for businesses and e-commerce software and services for the external sector. The second area, that is, web-enabled services include medical transcription, insurance claim processing, call centres. The third area is the hard-core e-business and e-trade services and projects which include B2C and B2B websites and portals as well as the e-business that Indian domestic companies had ventured into. E-trade includes initiatives where Indian trade and industry is transacting in export and import and the digital processes introduced inIndian regulatory bodies. In short, e-commerce industry is fast rising in India.

6.4 Reasons for Growth of E-commerce in India

6.4.1 Rising Middle Class: With the rise of small and medium enterprises, a new generation of globally minded Indian consumers has been created. Also, access to many global and domestic brands is limited to major metropolitan regions such as Delhi, Mumbai, and Bengaluru. Hence, the growing middle class is increasingly turning to e-commerce as the primary outlet for sophisticated consumer products and services.

6.4.2 Payment Gateways and Logistics: Lack of infrastructure is the largest challenges to e-commerce in India, complex interstate regulations and aversion of Indians to credit card is also a major hurdle in e- commerce ecosystem. However, a number of new payment gateway companies such as CC Avenue have helped in growth of e-commerce.

Alternative payment methods such as net banking and COD (cash on delivery) are now mandatory offerings for leading e-commerce platforms.

Paytm is one of the companies contributing to the growth of online payments. Alternative payments give consumers more options to pay and allow them to select payment methods that they are comfortable with. Language, domestic applications and familiarity with the payment method, coupled with the trust they place in their own bank, increases the usage. Consumers may use alternative payment methods due to security concerns with credit card purchases. Many alternative payments often require additional security steps, such as a user name, password or personal identification number (PIN) to further protect the consumer.

Cash on delivery can be seen as low risk option for consumers to enter e-commerce. However, it is a higher risk option for producers. Reliance on cash on delivery can act as an inhibitor of e-commerce growth due to people not playing when the product is delivered and to the lag between product dispatch and payment.

6.4.3 User Experience: E-commerce companies have invested in improving user experience such as merchandising, customer service, user interface design and guaranteed delivery and return policy which has led to an increase in the online consumers.

Endnote

1. Government of India, Ministry of Finance, *Budget Speech of the Finance Minister, 1994-95, Part B*, p. 24.

7

Foreign Direct Investment (FDI) in Services

Information and communication technology (ICT) is necessary to develop a country's productive capacity in all sectors of the economy. It links a country with the global economy and ensures competitiveness. In developed countries, there already exists a built up ICT capacity which causes inflow of FDI but in developing countries like India, ICT capacity has to be built up. In order to improve their ICT investments and benefit from anticipated increases in economic activity, developing countries are attracting foreign direct investment (FDI).

The ICT sector has been dynamic in many developed countries but in India it has its presence because of software exports. E-commerce sector has attracted huge investments.

7.1 What is Foreign Direct Investment (FDI)?

In pure economics, FDI is a direct investment into production or business in a country by an individual or company of another country, either by buying a company in the target country or by expanding operations of an existing business in that country. Foreign direct investment is in contrast to portfolio investment which is a passive investment in securities of another country such as stocks and bonds.

FDI is also described as "investment into the business of a country by a company in another country". Mostly, the investment is into production by either buying a company in the target country or by expanding operations of an existing business in that country". Such investments can take place for many reasons, including to take advantage of cheaper wages or special investment privileges (e.g. tax exemptions) offered by the country.

But the question arises as to why countries seek FDI? The answer may be:

1. Domestic capital is inadequate for purpose of economic growth.
2. Foreign capital is usually essential, at least as a temporary measure, during the period when the capital market is in the process of development.
3. Foreign capital usually brings with it other scarce productive factors like, technical know how, business expertise and knowledge.

The major benefits of FDI includes improvement in the foreign exchange (forex) position of the country, increase in exports, increases tax revenues, increase in production, employment generation and capital formation by bringing in fresh capital. It also helps in transfer of new technologies, management skills, intellectual property and increases competition within the local market and thus brings higher efficiencies.

But if there are such benefits attached to FDI, why is there opposition from local people?

1. The fear among domestic companies is that they may lose their ownership to overseas company.
2. Small enterprises fear that they may not be able to compete with world class large companies and may ultimately be edged out of business.
3. Large giants of the world try to monopolise and take over the highly profitablesectors.
4. Such foreign companies invest more in machinery and intellectual propertythan in wages of the local people.
5. Government has less control over the functioning of such companies as they usually work as wholly owned subsidiary of an overseas company.

7.2 Government Policy Regarding FDI

Foreign direct investment (FDI) is considered as a major source of non-debt financial resource for the economic development. FDI flows into India have grown consistently since liberalization and are an important component of foreign capital since FDI infuses long-term sustainable capital in the economy and contributes towards technology transfer, development of strategic sectors, greater innovation, competition and employment creation amongst other benefits. Therefore, it is the policy of the Government of India to attract and promote FDI in order to supplement domestic capital, technology and skills for accelerated economic growth and development. FDI, as distinguished from foreign portfolio investment, has the connotation of establishing a *lasting interest* in an enterprise that is resident in an economy other than that of the investor.

Foreign investment policy in the post-reforms period has emphasised greater encouragement and mobilisation of non-debt creating private inflows for reducing reliance on debt flows. Progressively liberal policies have led to increasing inflows of foreign investment in the country.

The initial policy stimulus to FDI in India came in July 1991 when the new industrial policy provided, *inter alia*, automatic approval for projects with foreign equity participation up to 51 percent in high priority areas. In recent years, the Government has initiated the second generation reforms under which measures have been taken to further facilitate and broaden the base of FDI in India. The policy for FDI allows freedom of location, choice of technology, repatriation of capital and dividends. As a result of these measures, there has been a strong surge of international interest in the Indian economy. The rate at which foreign direct investment inflow has grown during the post-liberalisation period is a clear indication that India is fast emerging as an attractive destination for overseas investors.

As part of the economic reforms programme, policy and procedures governing foreign investment and technology transfer have been significantly simplified and streamlined. Presently, foreign investment is freely allowed in all sectors including the services sector except in cases where there are sectoral ceilings.

It is the intent and objective of the Government of India to attract and promote foreign direct investment (FDI) in order to supplement domestic capital, technology and skills, for accelerated economic growth. FDI, as distinguished from portfolio investment, has the connotation of establishing a *lasting interest* in an enterprise that is resident in an economy other than that of the investor.

India has one of the most transparent and liberal FDI regimes among the emerging and developing economies. By FDI regime is meant those restrictions that apply to foreign nationals and entities but not to Indian nationals and Indian owned entities. The differential treatment is limited to a few entry rules, spelling out the proportion of equity that the foreign entrant can hold in an Indian (registered) company or business. There are a few banned sectors (like lotteries and gaming and legal services) and some sectors with limits on foreign equity proportion. The entry rules are clear and well-defined and equity limits for foreign investment in selected sectors such as telecom quite explicit and well-known.

7.3 Regulatory Framework

The government has put in place a policy framework on FDI, which is transparent, predictable and easily comprehensible. This framework is embodied in the Circular on Consolidated FDI Policy, which is updated from time-to-time to capture and keep pace with the regulatory changes, effected in the interregnum. Department for Promotion of Industry and Internal Trade (DPIIT), Ministry of Commerce and Industry, Government of India makes policy pronouncements on FDI through press notes/press releases which are notified by the Department of Economic Affairs (DEA), Ministry of Finance, Government of India as amendments to the Foreign Exchange Management (Non-Debt Instruments) Rules, 2019 under the Foreign Exchange Management Act, 1999 (42 of 1999) (FEMA). These notifications take effect from the date of issue of Press Notes/Press Releases, unless specified otherwise therein.

The payment of inward remittance and reporting

requirements are stipulated under the Foreign Exchange Management (Mode of Payment and Reporting of Non-Debt Instruments) Regulations, 2019 issued by the Reserve Bank of India (RBI). The regulatory framework, over a period of time, thus, consists of FEMA and Rules/Regulations thereunder, Consolidated FDI Policy Circular, press notes, press releases, clarifications, etc.

Consolidated FDI Policy Circular subsumes and supersedes all previous press notes/press releases, clarifications/circulars issued by DPIIT. The information given in this book is based on the Consolidated FDI Policy Circular which became effective from October 15, 2020.

7.4 Entities Eligible to Invest in India

These include the following:

1. A non-resident entity can invest in India, subject to the FDI Policy except in those sectors/activities which are prohibited. However, a citizen of Bangladesh or an entity incorporated in Bangladesh can invest only under the Government route. Further, a citizen of Pakistan or an entity incorporated in Pakistan can invest, only under the Government route, in sectors/activities other than defence, space and atomic energy and sectors/activities prohibited for foreign investment.
2. NRIs resident in Nepal and Bhutan as well as citizens of Nepal and Bhutan are permitted to invest in the capital of Indian companies on repatriation basis, subject to the condition that the amount of consideration for such investment shall be paid only by way of inward remittance in free foreign exchange through normal banking channels.
3. OCBs have been derecognized as a class of investors in India with effect from September 16, 2003. Erstwhile OCBs which are incorporated outside India and are not under the adverse notice of RBI can make fresh investments under FDI Policy as incorporated non-resident entities, with the prior approval of Government of India if

the investment is through Government route; and with the prior approval of RBI if the investment is through Automatic route.

4. A company, trust and partnership firm incorporated outside India and owned and controlled by NRIs can invest in India with the special dispensation as available to NRIs under the FDI Policy.
5. Foreign institutional investors (FIIs) and foreign portfolio investors (FPIs) may in terms of Schedule 2 and 2A of FEMA (Transfer or Issue of Security by Persons Resident Outside India) Regulations, as the case may be, respectively, invest in the capital of an Indian company under the Portfolio Investment Scheme which limits the individual holding of an FII/FPI below 10% of the capital of the company and the aggregate limit for FII/FPI investment to 24% of the capital of the company. This aggregate limit of 24% can be increased to the sectoral cap/statutory ceiling, as applicable, by the Indian company concerned through a resolution by its board of directors followed by a special resolution to that effect by its general body and subject to prior intimation to RBI. The aggregate FII/FPI investment, individually or in conjunction with other kinds of foreign investment, will not exceed sectoral/statutory cap.
6. Only registered FIIs/FPIs and NRIs as per Schedules 2,2A and 3 respectively of Foreign Exchange Management (Transfer or Issue of Security by a Person Resident Outside India) Regulations, 2000, can invest/trade through a registered broker in the capital of Indian Companies on recognised Indian Stock Exchanges.
7. A SEBI registered Foreign Venture Capital Investor (FVCI) may contribute up to 100% of the capital of an Indian company engaged in any activity mentioned in Schedule 6 of Notification No. FEMA 20/2000, including start-ups irrespective of the sector in which it is engaged, under the automatic route.
8. A non-resident Indian may subscribe to National Pension

System governed and administered by Pension Fund Regulatory and Development Authority (PFRDA), provided such subscriptions are made through normal banking channels and the person is eligible to invest as per the provisions of the PFRDA Act. The annuity/accumulated saving will be repatriable.

7.5 Prohibited Sectors

FDI is prohibited in the following sectors:

1. Lottery business including Government/private lottery, online lotteries etc.
2. Gambling and betting including casinos etc.
3. Chit funds.
4. Nidhi company.
5. Trading in transferable development rights (TDRs).
6. Real estate business or construction of farm houses. Real estate business shall not include development of townships, construction of residential/commercial premises, roads or bridges and Real Estate Investment Trusts (REITs) registered and regulated under the SEBI (REITs) Regulations 2014.
7. Manufacturing of cigars, cheroots, cigarillos and cigarettes, of tobacco or of tobacco substitutes.
8. Activities/sectors not open to private sector investment, e.g. atomic energy and railway operations (other than permitted activities).

Foreign technology collaboration in any form including licensing for franchise, trademark, brand name, management contract is also prohibited for lottery business and gambling and betting activities.

7.6 Permitted Sectors

Investments can be made by non-residents in the capital of a resident entity only to the extent of the percentage of the total capital as specified in the FDI policy. Investments by non-residents can be permitted in the capital of a resident entity in certain sectors/activity with entry conditions. Such conditions may include norms for minimum capitalization, lock-in period etc. Besides the entry conditions on foreign investment, the investment/investors are required to comply with all relevant sectoral laws, regulations, rules, security conditions, and state/ local laws/regulations.

Wherever there is a requirement of minimum capitalization, it shall include share premium received along with the face value of the share, only when it is received by the company upon issue of the shares to the non-resident investor. Amount paid by the transferee during post-issue transfer of shares beyond the issue price of the share, cannot be taken into account while calculating minimum capitalization requirement.

Sectoral cap, i.e. the maximum amount which can be invested by foreign investors in an entity, unless provided otherwise, is composite and includes all types of foreign investments, direct and indirect.

Foreign investment in sectors under government approval route resulting in transfer of ownership and/or control of Indian entities from resident Indian citizens to non-resident entities will be subject to government approval. Foreign investment in sectors under automatic route but with conditionalities, resulting in transfer of ownership and/or control of Indian entities from resident Indian citizens to non-resident entities, will be subject to compliance of such conditionalities.

Any existing foreign investment already made in accordance with the policy in existence would not require any modification to conform to amendments introduced.

The onus of compliance of above provisions will be on the investee company.

7.7 FDI in Services Sector

Since the early 1990s, the growth process in India has been marked by a remarkable performance of services sector. The experience of developed countries suggests that growth of services sector followed the growth of industrial sector. However, India's experience in this regard is somewhat different. The sectoral shift in favour of services sector over the last two decades has taken place in the face of an almost stagnant share of industry and a reduced share of agriculture in GDP. In fact, it was the growth performance of the services sector during the 1990s which sustained the overall growth of the Indian economy, particularly in times of adverse agricultural shocks and industrial slowdown.

The expansion of services has not only been conducive for employment generation but also for better efficiency of the system and better quality of life. Caps and conditions on FDI in the select services sector are listed in Table 7.1.

7.8 FDI in Financial Services

Financial sector of an economy is a multi-faceted term. It refers to the whole gamut of legal and institutional arrangements, financial intermediaries, markets and instruments with both domestic and external dimensions.

A well-functioning financial system is a pre-requisite for the pursuit of economic growth with stability. The core function of a financial system is to facilitate smooth and efficient allocation of resources from savers to the ultimate users. The financial infrastructure contributes to the effective functioning of institutions and markets and thereby to stability. Hence, it serves as the foundation for adequate access to financial services and sustained financial development.

No major economy in the world today can be viewed in isolation from the rest of the world. Given the size and the growing magnitude of interaction—in terms of trade, services, and capital flows—and the greater openness to globalisation, India is in a different economic milieu today than it was two decades ago. India is virtually part of the world of globalised finance and is learning to walk, negotiating the strong currents, both positive and negative, generated by the forces of financial globalisation.

FDI in financial services is indicated in Table 7.2.

Table 7.1: FDI in Select Services Sector

Sector/Activity	Percent of equity/FDI Cap	Entry Route
1. Broadcasting		
A. Broadcasting Carriage Services		
Teleports, cable networks, mobile TV and other services.	100%	Automatic
B. Broadcasting Content Services		
Terrestrial broadcasting FM (FM Radio) and up-linking of news and current affairs TV channels	49%	Government
Up-linking of non-news and current affairs TV channels/down-linking of TV channels	100%	Automatic
2. Print Media		
A. Publishing of newspaper and periodicals dealing with news and current affairs B. Publication of Indian editions of foreign magazines dealing with news and current affairs	26%	Government
C. Publishing/printing of scientific and technical magazines/specialty journals/periodicals, subject to specified conditions. D. Publication of facsimile edition of foreign newspapers	100%	Government
3. Construction Development: Townships, Housing, Built-up Infrastructure	100%	Automatic
4. Industrial Parks: New and Existing	100%	Automatic
5. Satellites: Establishment and Operation	100%	Government

Source: Government of India, Ministry of Commerce and Industry, Department for Promotion of Industry and Internal Trade (DPIIT), *Consolidated FDI Policy* (effective from October 15, 2020).

Table 7.2: FDI in Financial Services

Sector/Activity	Percent of equity/FDI Cap	Entry Route
1. Asset Reconstruction Companies	100%	Automatic
2. Banking–Private sector	74%	Automatic up to 49%. Government route beyond 49% and up to 74%.
3. Banking-Public Sector	20%	Government
4. Credit Information Companies (CIC).	100%	Automatic
5. Infrastructure Companies in Securities Markets		
Infrastructure companies in securities markets, namely, stock exchanges, depositories and clearing corporations, in compliance with SEBI Regulations.	49%	Automatic
6. Insurance		
Insurance company.	49%	Automatic
Insurance intermediaries	100%	Automatic
7. Pension Sector	49%	Automatic
8. Power Exchanges	49%	Automatic
9. White Label ATM Operations	100%	Automatic
10. Other Financial Services	100%	Automatic

Source: Same as for Table 7.1.

8

E-commerce Retailers in India

8.1 Origin and Growth of E-commerce in India

E-commerce in India is two decades old but major developments have occurred since 2010. It all began in 2002 with online travel sites like IRCTC and makemytrip.com which changed the way Indians booked travel tickets. There were several factors which have led to a conducive environment for e-commerce to flourish such as increase in internet user base, increase in smart phone penetration and alternative payment systems. Marketers can promote their products and services using internet, covering greater geographical areas. Companies such as Groupon (offers deal on travel, selected electronics, fashion), Gilt (flash sales on designer label collections), Fab (Flash sales of selected products) and RetailMeNot (digital coupans from retailers and brands) are collaborating with daily deals and discount sites so as to encash upon the opportunity of increasing trend of online shopping.

Home grown players like Flipkart and Snapdeal have shown tremendous growth and attracted some big investors. Since, it is a capital-intensive business and to build a large e-commerce business, capital is required. Big quantum of investments has been made in Indian e-commerce industry as investors are trying to cash in on the opportunity.

E-commerce market in India has become crowded and complex with several players fighting for a fair share of customers. As there is intense competition in the e-commerce market, the companies are using multiple business models in order to get customer attention.

Further, to survive and sustain operations in the competitive market, companies are also taking advantage of one or multiple revenue models and follow one of the two business models viz. vertical focused or multi-category. Vertical focused players cater to a particular sector such as garments and food. Another form of differentiation is market place model versus inventory-led model. In the market place model, online retail website works as a channel between sellers and buyers. In inventory-led model, online retail stores keep stocks in warehouses and sell themselves.

8.2 Modus Operandi of Online Retailers

The modus operandi of e-commerce companies is to simply try and get a lot of new users to try out their platform and also rely on the fact that their platform is user friendly. These companies also make sure that consumers like what they see and also make sure that the customers are satisfied with the goods. Last but not the least, since there are a lot of players competing with each other, they also need to provide the cheapest pricing for the best products.

E-commerce companies including Flipkart, Amazon and Snapdeal are funding discounts on their sites using complex mechanisms.

The three major e-commerce companies operating in India include Flipkart, Amazon and Snapdeal, with all of them operating as market places. That is primarily because Indian laws do not allow FDI in e-commerce sites that sell directly to customers, but allows it in marketplaces that link sellers and buyers. The marketplaces also provide services such as payment, storage and delivery.

As direct retail is banned, marketplaces are not allowed to exercise control over the product prices of the sellers on their platforms, including on matters concerning discounts.

Yet, Flipkart, Amazon and Snapdeal do actually have a significant say in deciding product prices as all the three sites finance part and, in some cases, the full amount of discounts offered by sellers albeit in an indirect manner.

Mint lists some of the ways in which the three sites,

Amazon, Flipkart and Snapdeal fund discounts on their sites.

8.2.1 Amazon: After comparing prices with other sites, Amazon recommends the amount of discounts to its sellers on products, but doesn't force them to adopt these suggested prices. Sellers, however, end up keeping these suggested prices because Amazon finances the discounts. This is how it works: at the end of a certain period, sellers send a debit note to Amazon titled "promotional funding". This note contains the amountof discount that the seller gave on apparel, electronics, toys and other products sold on the site. Amazon then pays the seller by cheque and in some cases, also gives additional money as the seller's margin. This debit note is over and above what Amazon collects from the customer.

8.2.2 Flipkart: WS Retail Services Pvt. Ltd, a seller on Flipkart, accounts for more than 75 percent of the site's sales. For products sold by WS Retail, Flipkart does not fund discounts. However, with other sellers, Flipkart suggests prices but unlike Amazon does not typically pay the amount of discounts to sellers by cheque. Instead, it forgoes commissions or listing fees it charges its sellers.

During Flipkart's recent Big Billion Day sale, many of the sellers apart from WS Retail were simply promised a certain amount and discounts were almost entirely funded by Flipkart. Sellers were paid through bank transfer by Flipkart.

8.2.3 Snapdeal: Like Amazon, Snapdeal also finances part or full discounts given by most of its sellers. Snapdeal pays sellers by real time gross settlement (RTGS), a form of internet banking, or by cheque. Snapdeal refers to the discounts as "promotional expenses". During Snapdeal's recent Buy One, Get One promotional offer, sellers were paid for both products by Snapdeal, which charged its commission fee only on one item. The discounting process highlights how these sites spend huge amount of money that they have raised from investors, or in Amazon's case, received from its parent company.

As of now, e-commerce companies are focusing on customer acquisition and increasing market cap and not looking for profit.

They are able to manage it because of the funding from different investors. Jabong has its own logistics fleet across major metros and few other smaller cities in India. E-commerce companies such as Flipkart, Amazon, Snapdeal, Ebay deliver more than a million merchandises in metro cities such as Mumbai, Chennai, Bengaluru, and Delhi alone. E-commerce companies outsource the logistics and delivery work to private players such as BlueDart, DTDC, Professional Couriers, FedEx, DHL and few others to handle cash on delivery (COD) service for them. Many metros have small courier companies with whom e-commerce companies tie up for COD service and some charge an additional fee for cash collection.

8.3 Difference between Alibaba and Amazon

Alibaba's goal is to help small businesses stand in contrast to Amazon, who is often (fairly or otherwise) criticized for making it harder for small businesses to compete and stay online.

The business model which Alibaba follows is that of platform model that merely facilitate the transactions. It manages the marketplace and charge a sales commission, but don't hold or sell any merchandise itself.

Amazon, by comparison, operates in both inventory and marketplace model. On Amazon.com, there are thousands of products one can buy directly from third party businesses. But Amazon is also in the business of stocking items and selling the products directly to consumers. That means in many instances, it is competing directly with the same merchants who are using its platform to sell. Also, it has to deal with all the logistically complex and expensive physical aspects such as building vast warehouse network.

It is this difference that explains why Alibaba is profitable, while Amazon has random fluctuations in its profits. Alibaba's business within China is 84 percent and 16 percent internationally whereas Amazon's business from North America is 60 percent and 40 percent outside North America.

Alibaba has a stranglehold on the Chinese market and Amazon is the undisputed US leader (Source: Andrew, 2014).

8.4 Lessons for India

Alibaba is known for building an e-commerce network in a developing nation and making it a lifestyle statement for Chinese consumers. In various aspects, China and India are quite similar and Alibaba's success holds useful lessons for India. There seems to be lot to learn for Flipkart, Snapdeal and others to become the Alibaba of India.

One of the biggest hurdles is internet penetration. Expanding India's high-speed internet and communication infrastructure would also be critical. A major reason for China's e-commerce success is that internet adoption has spread faster than brick and mortar stores. The country's massive size and huge population means that many foreign brands remain confined to China's largest cities (Apple, for example, has only 12 stores in China). People in smaller cities and China's less developed regions have taken to online shopping, using the internet to buy higher quality and more diverse goods online. For e-commerce to have the same impact in India, internet infrastructure must expand significantly as according to the International Telecommunications Union (ITU), only 14 percent of India's population had access to the internet, compared to nearly 46 percent in China.

One of the crucial lessons that have to be learnt from Alibaba is creating opportunities for others, which in turn helps one grow as it does not hold inventory and deliver goods itself. In fact, it is a link between merchants, customers, and logistics firms that helps it achieve the large sales number.

It is quite crucial to reach small towns and traditional businesses in India so that it can grow. Taking a cue from Alibaba, Flipkart started a pilot project to link India's small and traditional businesses with its 22 million customers online. After raising $1 billion fresh funding in July 2014, the company launched an initiative called "Flipkart Kaarigar Ka

Dwaar" to add weavers in the north-eastern Indian city of Varanasi to its site. By connecting small businesses to the global market place, it could help to breed a new entrepreneurial class and create jobs and opportunities. It teamed up with the Textiles Ministry to provide an online marketing platform for handloom weavers across the country.

This model would be especially powerful in India, where almost 51 percent of the workforce is self-employed. A technology-driven consumer-to-consumer ecosystem could connect millions of India's small and medium enterprises (SMEs) to the formal economy, and also lead to the growth of new industries and higher living standards in rural villages, as it has been achieved in China.

India can learn from another aspect of Alibaba, that is, its provision of various financial services to small businesses. Faced with the problem of buyers trusting the merchants on its site, Alibaba created an innovative payment system named Alipay in 2004. Alipay protects buyers against potential fraud by holding payment in escrow until the customer receives the goods and can verify that they are real. The payment tool helped to build confidence in e-commerce in China and remained key to the platform's success. In fiscal 2014, nearly 80 percent of Alibaba's retail transactions were done through this service.

From Alipay, Alibaba gradually expanded into other financial services. It launched its own SME lending operation, aimed at supporting small companies to join its internet platform. The company also opened a money-market fund, named Yu'EBao or "Leftover Treasure", that allows users to invest surplus cash in their Alipay accounts. Since, it offers high interest rates and no minimum investment, the service has been widely popular and went on to become the largest money market fund in China.

By supporting the entrepreneurs that make up its platform, these financial services helped Alibaba itself to grow. It gave access to a vast amount of information on Chinese small businesses, their creditworthiness, and the volume of their online transactions. It also quickened the pace of financial intermediation in China. This model could be replicated in India to help policymakers achieve the goal of expanding the access of small businesses to financial services. In his budget speech in 2015, India's Finance Minister Arun Jaitley proposed setting up a US$ 1.6 billion fund to attract private capital for small and medium enterprises (SMEs). However, the bigger challenge would be to allocate this capital efficiently to create valuable businesses, especially when little is known about the creditworthiness of small companies. In India, the e-commerce industry could find similar resources but it all depends on how they are utilised as it is a mix of technological advancement, creating opportunities and building trust.

8.5 Conclusion

The success of Alibaba in China suggests that with a relatively large population, a certain scale is helpful for the growth of e-commerce and also for the presence of localized e-commerce platform.

As already discussed, all the e-commerce companies in India are making losses and how they are funding discounts by burning cash out of venture capital (VC) funding. There is no differentiation among firms other than discounts but it cannot be a long-term strategy for these firms. The challenge for these firms is to devise a strategy whereby the consumers buy at a non-discounted price and yet the customer loyalty is maintained. E-commerce companies have been forced to do a reality check as there is pressure from the investors to turn it into a profitable business. The VC/seed investors believe that the strategy of giving huge discounts while earning wafer-thin margins is spoiling the e-commerce game in India. In fact, VC funding is not required to start business, but to scale business and ensure profits.

A popular music streaming services player Dhingana.com posted a message on its site. It read: "Goodbye! All good things must come to an end. We thank you from the bottom of our hearts for letting us be a part of your musical moments". The "Goodbye" message paints a grim picture of the e-commerce space in India, backed by venture capitalists (VCs) and seed investors.

There are many ways in which producers may offer and deliver their products to consumers. There are several ways of co-operation between producers and retailers depending on the sales channel and the party responsible for delivery. When introducing direct online sales to consumers, the number of options is further extended. Moreover different (online and offline) business models can be combined. For example, in the traditional retail model, sales are done at the retail shop and the consumer picks up the products at the retail shop. In this situation, the producer delivers the products to the retailer and in 'producer's web shop' the sales are done via the web shop of the producer and the producer also does home delivery. The retailer is not a part of the supply chain in the 'producer's web shop' model.

E-commerce impacts the supply chain of the producers in electronics. This impact increases when producers are selling to consumers online and are also delivering to consumers themselves ('producer's web shop model'). For producers, this results in a complex supply chain, based on aspects like shorter product lifecycles, separated picking strategies/stocks, smaller order sizes, higher number of deliveries, differentiation in packaging, and internationalization. These changes create a significant challenge for e-commerce retailers to remain profitable while meeting consumer's expectations. The most important driver for the choice for one or more e-commerce business models is customer value. Also, the COD method and high rates of return is big hurdle in e-commerce.

The issues among e-commerce firms include bad business model (low margins, high customer acquisition cost, huge discount), and extremely low levels of differentiation (selling same brands as available on all places while competing on price). As most e-commerce firms are closely held private companies and in the absence of any credible figures on earnings and revenue arriving at their valuation is a difficult task. With the e-commerce companies not turning profitable, VCs can make an exit through selling off the business. Completely online marketplace model is not going to work in India. Hybrid model like online + offline, online + kiosk, and online + offline agents, would better work in India.

9

Alibaba

Alibaba, the world's business giant in e-commerce market, started with a small idea and a vision based on observing the early success of ebay and Amazon in US. By understanding the needs of the people in the Chinese society, Alibaba has been selling the services that cater to their requirements. Three major web portals make up the core of Alibaba's business: Alibaba, Taobao, and Tmall. All three of these e-commerce websites serve to connect various types of buyers and sellers, wherein Alibaba acts as a middleman.

Alibaba Group provides three online business to business marketplaces that connect buyers and sellers from around the world, that is, an English language marketplace (alibaba.com), a Chinese language marketplace (alibaba.com.cn) and a Japanese language marketplace (alibaba.co.jp).

9.1 E-commerce Websites

9.1.1 Alibaba: Alibaba.com was launched in 1999 in Hangzhou by Jack Ma, a former English teacher, along with a group of 17 friends. It is a business to business (B2B) trading platform, connecting manufacturers from countries such as China, India, Pakistan, the United States and Thailand with international buyers. Merchants can list their products for free on Alibaba.com, but also have the option to pay for a range of benefits such as greater exposure on the site and unlimited product listings.

9.1.2 Taobao: In Chinese, Taobao means "search for treasure". It was launched in 2003, and it lists large number of products and services from many sellers. Taobao doesn't charge transaction fees and the site is free to join for merchants, a policy which helped the site gain its enormous user base in China.

Taobao.com has grown to become China's largest shopping website and is ranked the ninth most popular website in the world by Alexa.com. While Alibaba.com is business to business (B2B), Taobao is business to consumer (B2C) or consumer to consumer (C2C) focused, enabling small businesses and individuals to open online stores. In Taobao, advertisers can choose between pay for performance and display marketing and through these advertisements, Alibaba makes money from Taobao.

9.1.3 Tmall: Tmall.com was launched in 2008 offering a wide selection of branded products which are oriented towards China's growing middle class. While Taobao caters more to small merchants and individuals as sellers, Tmall is focused on larger companies, including multinational brands such as Nike and Apple. Tmall charges merchants a deposit, an annual fee, and a commission fee on transactions. In this way, it bears some resemblance to eBay and Amazon, which also collect transaction fees from third-party merchants. Sellers on Tmall have access to analytic tools showing the number of visitors, page views, and customer ratings, which serve to help guide their business decisions.

9.2 Ecosystem of Alibaba Group

In addition to its leading e-commerce portals, Alibaba Group created an ecosystem of companies to compliment them.

9.2.1 Alipay: Alipay is an online third party payment platform, launched in 2004 by Alibaba Group. It provides payments and escrow services (releasing money to sellers only once their buyers are happy with the goods received) for transactions on Alibaba Group platforms. However, Alibaba Group spun off Alipay in 2010.

In 2010, the People's Bank of China (PBoC) issued new rules regarding third-party online payment companies in which they must apply and receive licenses from the PBoC in order to operate. So, Jack Ma spun off Alipay under another company.

9.2.2 Alimama: Alimama, launched in November 2007, is an online marketing platform that provides sellers on Alibaba Group's marketplaces, a range of marketing and advertising services.

9.2.3 China Smart Logistics: China Smart Logistics is a proprietary platform that provides real-time access to information for both buyers and sellers with a view to improving the efficiency of e-commerce package deliveries.

9.2.4 Aliyun: Aliyun develops platforms for cloud computing (cloud computing is a model for delivering information technology services in which resources are retrieved from the internet through web-based tools and applications, rather than a direct connection to a server) and data management, ensuring that Alibaba's e-commerce portals can handle their massive traffic and transaction volumes.

This diversification of Alibaba group to other web services helped in expanding its business portfolio to include services like retail websites and business management solutions, thereby, making it one of the largest and most comprehensive providers of internet retail and B2B services. These sites enable Chinese and foreign firms to trade everything from automobiles, building materials, iPods, TVs and stationery.

9.3 Role of Alibaba in Rural E-commerce

China had recognized potential of e-commerce as it has a rural population of over 650 million of which about 165 million have internet access and Central Government had taken numerous measures to reduce the urban-rural digital divide. Rural e-commerce initiative may be illustrated by two examples of Rural Jiangsu and Zhejiang provinces.

In Suichang, a county with the population of 50,000 in the Zhejiang provinces, villagers in 2005 started selling agricultural products (vegetables, tea, herbs, bamboo etc.) through Alibaba e-commerce portal. The household had setup stores with annual sales exceeding Yuan 120 million ($19

Million) by 2012. The increased sales helped the villagers to revital the upstream crop farming such as the size of bamboo forest more than double. Operation of online store in the village resulted in increased in employment and was estimated to exceed 3,000 and the number of online stores in Suichang had grown to about 1,500. The online shop association was setup in 2010 which helped the villagers in training and transfer of knowledge and logistics. Regular course on how to operate an online store were made available to villagers free of charge.

An agreement was made between Suichang County and TaoBao.com, the C2C online market place of the Alibaba group in May 2012 to establish a dedicated portal viz. suichang.china.taobao.com. As a result of this, most of the Suichang e-commerce merchants had setup online source on this market place.

The local Government upgraded transport conditions so that the village could link to remote areas and to China's superhighway network.

9.4 Alibaba and Baidu

The element of Alibaba's business strategy lies in its relationship with Baidu, which operates China's leading search engine. Alibaba actually blocks Baidu's spider from indexing both Taobao and Tmall, meaning that pages from these websites do not appear in Baidu's search results. Hence, shoppers must go directly to Taobao and Tmall in order to see what these sites are offering and when customer is making a search on Taobao and Tmall, advertisement from merchants appear alongside search results. This aspect of Alibaba's business model is similar to Google, which makes the majority of its revenue through online advertising.

As a result, consumer behaviour in China has effectively shifted to evade third party search sites when shopping online. This is beneficial for sellers as Alibaba sites have become a singular force in consumer discovery, consideration and purchase. In theory, this would also create efficiencies for search and display advertisements, with multiple touch points on one platform.

9.5 Business Model

The initial business model of Alibaba was simple—to facilitate a 24x7 meeting platform for suppliers and buyers around the world. From the start, Alibaba did not just connect Chinese suppliers with international buyers, but it had the goal of connecting all importers and exporters around the world with each other.

Alibaba follows the platform model as its business model that merely facilitates the transactions. It manages the marketplace and charges a sales commission. It also generates revenue from deposits and annual user fees are charged from retailers utilizing the site. Alibaba also generates revenue from its micro-lending business that caters to individual borrowers. However, Taobao, operates as a fee marketplace where neither sellers nor buyers are assessed a fee for completing transactions but, sellers have the option to buy advertising and other services to help them stand out on the website and boost sales. Advertisers can choose between pay for performance and display marketing and these advertisements are the source through which Alibaba makes money from Taobao.

9.6 Market Strategy

Alibaba.com is playing an important role in helping SMEs in China and around the world participate in global trade and become more competitive at the global level. As a leading company, Alibaba.com is researching, developing and creating new concepts answering to new needs and focusing primarily on customer's expectations, enabling it to know how to capture market opportunities and to expand its strategy to the SMEs overall growth throughout the world. It aims to make business less complex for SMEs all over the world and it has been successful in doing so till now.

The four Ps, i.e. product, price, promotion and place distribution have contributed to the success of Alibaba.com on business to business marketing.

9.6.1 Product/Service Strategy: Alibaba.com offers variety of services (perception of the consumer or the user) such as trust and safety through account protection tutorials to both buyers and the sellers and to report disputes between buyers and sellers to Alibaba.com, if they may arise. Online payment is secured with an escrow as discussed earlier. It also offers listing solutions, protection and authentication, and instant messaging. Alibaba.com has a trade manager where buyers and suppliers can chat and trade instantly. Suppliers using the trade manager can send product photos or file of any size in an instant. Alibaba.com has after sales services such as a warranty program whereby buyers get up to one year warranty in case of a breakdown, mainly for electronic products.

This will help consumers to have access to more suppliers, and less risk of fraud with the availability of escrow service since the website would not make payment to the seller until the delivery has been confirmed by the buyers, which in turns helps in checking whether the customers are happy with the goods or not.

The sellers don't have to pay Taobao to set up internet store, so given the low set-up cost, Taobao attracts many people willing to give it a try and sell variety of products. The sellers will have access to many buyers as variety of products is being sold at Taobao which increases the availability of merchandise and generates traffic at the website.

9.6.2 Pricing Strategy: Alibaba Group has adopted a number of pricing strategies including competition pricing, i.e. setting a price in comparison with the competitors. Alibaba Group uses competitive pricing so that the price offered by it does not differ much from that of its competitors.

Discount is another way of pricing used by the Alibaba Group. The company chose this method because it stimulates sales while retaining customers. Discounts by Alibaba are given to customers when they buy products in bulk and during the festival season. Some suppliers use the BOGOF (buy one get one free) method. Alibaba Group offers the product to consumers at a lower price but adds service charges such as shipping charges, fast delivery, guarantees, warranties, custom design which may increase the price and this method is adopted to ensure that the total cost of the products together with the value added services is more than the production cost so that the company can earn profit.

Since Alibaba had a historical advantage of head start, it has an edge over its competitors. Alibaba has made efforts to block major search sites, mainly Baidu. As a result, consumer behaviour in China has effectively shifted to evade third party search sites when shopping online and it provides customers outstanding value and superior shopping experience.

9.6.3 Promotion Strategy: Promotion is a term used to describe the advertising, promotion, publicity and selling of a product or service. Promotion aims at creating awareness about the organization's products or services to the target market. Promotion can be broken down into two distinct categories: face to face selling and advertising, and promotion and publicity.

Alibaba.com uses the internet promotion strategy because internet is a cost effective and fastest promotion tool. The presence of Alibaba.com company profile and product/services in major search engines like Yahoo gives it a global exposure and creates awareness among buyers/sellers.

Alibaba.com uses various campaign taglines during its promotions. Examples of taglines used are: "Find it, make it, sell it"; "Draw up your business plan. Lock down your prototype". Alibaba used catchy slogans to include more sellers as it works on characteristic of inclusion and slowly diversified and added new customers from different arenas.

Alibaba.com has also promoted its product/services through sponsoring of events such as Australia-China Business Week,

Beijing Olympics etc. Since, Olympics are a major international event and by making its presence felt, it had increased the brand image for its existing customers.

9.6.4 Place/Distribution Strategy: Place refers to a general concept describing how the product will get to the consumers. Place includes all of the targeted market outlets and distribution tactics needed to deliver the product for sale to consumers. The channel of distribution involves the logistics, wholesalers and other intermediaries. Efficient distribution is very essential in achieving the company's marketing objective.

Alibaba Group has several online B2B marketplaces from where potential buyers and suppliers from around the world can obtain its products and services.

Other B2B sites offered by Alibaba Group in six non-English language which can help native traders source products online easily are:

1. Spanish: http://spanish.alibaba.com,
2. German: http://german.alibaba.com
3. Italian: http://italian.alibaba.com
4. French: http://french.alibaba.com
5. Portuguese: http://portuguese.alibaba.com
6. Russian: http://russian.alibaba.com

Dedicated logistics and warehousing support has ensured timely delivery to the consumers. Alibaba has empowered small businesses by helping them to connect with new customers in China and the rest of the world, thus, providing faster information, faster access and ease of business.

Alibaba has made numerous investments in technology companies over the past few years, but many appear to be for the purpose of appealing to investors rather than for making money. The company's movie production company had never made money, and its attempt at challenging YouTube's video hosting dominance, YoukuTudou, lost US$ 140 million in 2014. The cloud computing company Aliyun received US$ 1 billion from the parent company in 2015, but it does not appear to have made any money either.

9.7 Revenue Stream

For the financial year ending March 31, 2020, Alibaba Group recorded consolidated revenue of around 717.3 billion Yuan (approximately US$ 109 billion).

Overall, the largest portion of Alibaba Group's revenue is generated through Chinese-based e-commerce which reached a staggering 473.7 billion Yuan in 2021. In 2021, retail e-commerce in China accounted for 66 percent of company's revenue. International commerce retail netted 34.5 billion Yuan of annual revenues.

Alibaba's Chinese retail marketplace had around 811 million annual active buyers.

9.8 Conclusion

Alibaba acts as a middleman between buyers and sellers online and facilitates the sale of goods between the two parties through its extensive network of websites. Taobao operates as a fee marketplace where neither sellers nor buyers are charged a fee for completing transactions. But, as an internal search engine, it generates advertising revenue for Alibaba that resembles Google's core business model. Alibaba created Alipay which resembles PayPal, following the concerns of customers over the security and validity of transactions completed online. As a secure payment system, Alipay protects buyers in the event sellers are unable to or refuse to deliver goods sold.

The four Ps of the marketing strategies have also contributed to the success of Alibaba.com. It has been able to emerge as a grand business to business site where customers can easily obtain products and services from a wide range of products available. The rise of Alibaba can be attributed to its local knowledge and understanding of the local buyers and sellers. Hence, with right marketing strategies, Alibaba.com has been able to reach the targeted customers thereby fulfilling their needs accordingly.

10

Amazon and Jabong

10.1 Amazon

Amazon was launched in India in 2013 and it has become a significant player in the country's e-commerce market. According to Royal Bank of Canada, "Amazon's efforts in India could potentially start to positively impact the company's overall gross profit growth by 2018" (Dutta, 2015).

10.1.1 Revenue Model: Amazon operates through both inventory model and marketplace model. On Amazon.com, there are thousands of products one can buy directly from third party businesses. But Amazon is also in the business of stocking items and selling products directly to consumers. That means in many instances, it is competing directly with the same merchants who are using its platform to sell. It charges a portion of the sales price as commission.

Amazon also operates through subscription-based revenue model through its Amazon Prime service. Under a Prime account, customers pay an annual fee to secure free two day or same day shipping on eligible items and an annual fee to have access to digital music or movies. Amazon also generates revenue from selling its e-reader, Kindle and the e-book and mobile application purchases offered to Kindle owners.

However, India's contribution to Amazon's global revenues is minuscule at the moment. In 2020, Germany was the most lucrative international market for the company with a share of 7.7 percent of the total revenues, followed by UK at 6.9 percent and Japan at 5.3 percent. Share of revenues from the rest of the world including India stood at 11.9 percent in 2020.

But Amazon, like the rest of the industry, probably realizes that these are still early days for online commerce in India, which means that potentially there is immense room for growth. Selling expenses as percentage of sales came down from approximately 1/6th of the sale in 2011 to 1/3rd of the sales in 2015. Decrease in selling expenses as percentage of sales may be the result of many factors including fall in cost of advertising, fall in sales commission, and fall in transportation costs or carriage outward. Although, fall in selling expenses would lead to higher net profit for the firm, yet the firm has to ensure that there is no decline in the publicity/goodwill in the market.

10.1.2 Expansion in India: In July 2014, Amazon founder Jeff Bezos announced that the online retailer would invest US$ 2 billion in its India business. The online retail giant has committed investments worth US$ 6.5 billion in the country to date. During his visit to India, Jeff Bezos opined, "I predict the 21st century will be the Indian century. This country has dynamism and energy and everywhere I go here we see there is an improvement in growth. This country has something special".

While on an expansion spree, Amazon and private equity firm Samara Capital jointly acquired Aditya Birla Group's grocery retail chain "More" for ₹ 4,050 crore in September 2018. They invested a further ₹ 275 crore in the venture in September 2020.

Amazon also entered into an agreement to acquire 49 percent stake in Future Coupons, a promoter entity of Future Retail in August 2019 for around ₹ 1,500 crore. Amazon is currently involved in an ongoing court tussle with Future Group and Reliance Industries after the latter acquired Future Group's retail and wholesale business.

Amazon India has also made a commitment to induct 10,000 electric vehicles into its delivery fleet by 2025.

Hence, it is expanding in India at a much faster rate than any of its other markets. Also, it is working towards strengthening its logistics. The company has set up its own logistics company to directly deliver goods to its customers. Amazon has also partnered with India Post, one of the world's largest postal networks to help it reach deeper into the hinterland.

Amazon hopes that India will become its largest overseas market but there is competition from Flipkart. It has to formulate a policy of scaling up rather than just following aggressive price policy like other e-commerce firms. As discussed, its profit pattern is quite random and solvency ratios (debt/equity and QR) are indicating warning signs. Like in US, it was involved in tax related issue with Karnataka Tax Authorities whereby Amazon India has been stopped from selling some products from its warehouse in the state by cancelling the license of third-party merchants who supply goods to the Amazon's Karnataka warehouse (Source: Asthana, 2014).

10.2 Jabong

Jabong.com is a part of the German Rocket Internet Group and is an Indian fashion and lifestyle e-commerce portal, headquartered at Gurgaon, NCR and started its operations in January 2012. The company received around 14,000 orders daily (Agarwal, 2013) and offered more than 90,000 products on the site (Ranjan, 2013). Jabong was one of the most visited e-commerce sites during the Great Online Shopping Festival, 2013 (Sharma, 2013). Company representatives claimed that its revenues increased five to six times compared to a usual day and that Jabong had set a record for sale in the male fashion category.

10.2.1 Business Model: Jabong.com follows both an inventory model and a managed marketplace model (Gulati, 2013). In the inventory model, products are sourced from brands and stored in the Jabong warehouse. In the managed marketplace model, Jabong provides marketing, logistics and delivery (Hector, 2013).

10.2.3 International Store: Jabong also has an international online shopping store called Jabongworld.com, which sells Indian ethnic wear such as sarees, lehengas, salwar suits and dress materials. Jabongworld.com has also introduced its Indo-Western wear range, priced in foreign currencies.

It receives highest amount of website traffic from United States, closely followed by Malaysia and Mauritius and other countries. According to The Brand Trust Report India Study, 2013 by Trust Research Advisory, Jabong ranked among the top 25 trusted online brands in India (exchange4media).

Jabong is among the top 3 ecommerce players in India when it comes to customer satisfaction and won the "Online Retailer of the Year" award in the first e-Tailing India E-Commerce Industry Awards.

With increased use of smart phones and internet, Jabong had adopted a new approach that has enhanced the shopping experience of customers. Jabong introduced its mobile application in April 2014 and received about 27 percent of all orders from mobile devices in the second quarter of 2014. This increased by about 60 percent by the end of 2014.

The company received 62 percent orders from tier-2 and tier-3 cities. Increased usage of smart phones and lack of branded showrooms in the cities were considered as prime factors that contributed to the growth of mobile shopping for the e-commerce portal.

Research had shown that the most interesting factor in the growth of e-commerce portals is that mobile applications are the key to their success as it offers the comfort of purchasing from anywhere and getting it delivered at their preferred destination.

There seems to be direct relation between new customers signing up on Jabong and growth in orders placed, when customer base increased at a double digit rate throughout 2013, so did its orders placed. However with increase in customer base down to single digits, order growth is also down to single digits. It is worth noting that there are seasonal changes in demand which could have affected sales growth.

10.2.4 Unique Visitor and Conversion Ratio: Unique visitor is defined as a person who visits a site at least once within the reporting period. Even if the same IP address accesses the site many times, it still only counts as one visitor during the reported period. In e-commerce, the conversion marketing is to convert the site visitor into paying customers. The unique visitor and conversion ratio for Jabong was near to 1 percent always, which implies that the company needed to focus on its customer services such as feedback about products and services, and identification of visitors interested in particular products or services, based on previous site browsing.

Jabong has a total warehouse capacity of 215,000 square feet, with delivery service to over 12,000 pin codes across India, including 630 cities. Jabong also had a logistics arm called JAVAS that has been sold.

Jabong is currently the only loss making business in terms of gross profit in Rocket Internet's Global Fashion Group. As discussed earlier, it should focus on improving customer services in terms of trust, logistics, technology and move to marketplace model so that inventories are not piled up. The discrepancy in data raises doubts about the credentials of the figures reported by the company. In the absence of credible figures on revenue and earnings, valuation becomes difficult.

11

Snapdeal and Flipkart

11.1 Snapdeal

In 2010, when Kunal Bahl and Rohit Bansal wanted to start their own business, they chose an offline couponing business and named it Money Saver. 15,000 coupons were sold in three months and it was time to take the business to the next level. It was after they met investor Vani Kola that the venture really took off.

Initially started as an offline business, Snapdeal went online in 2010. At that point of time, eBay was the only marketplace in India. Snapdeal had grown to become the largest online marketplace in India offering 30 million plus products from more than 275,000 sellers with a reach to more than 6,000 towns and cities across India.

11.1.1 Acquisitions:

1. In June 2011, Snapdeal acquired Bengaluru based group buying site, Grabbon.com (The Financial Express, 2010).
2. In April 2012, Snapdeal acquired esportsbuy.com, an online sports goods retailer based out of Delhi (Chatterjee, 2012).
3. In May 2013, Snapdeal acquired Shopo.in, an online marketplace for Indianhandicraft products (Times of India, 2013).
4. In April 2014, Snapdeal acquired fashion products discovery site, Doozton.com (The Economic Times, 2014).
5. In December 2014, Snapdeal acquired gifting recommendation site, Wishpicker.com (The Economic Times, 2014).
6. In January 2015, Snapdeal acquired a stake in product comparison website Smartprix.com (Peer, 2015).
7. In February 2015, Snapdeal acquired luxury fashion products

discovery site, Exclusively.in (Business Standard, 2015).

8. In March 2015, Snapdeal acquired a 20 percent stake in logistics service company Gojavas.com. It owns a 50 percent stake in GoJavas valued at US$ 35 million (Verma, 2015).
9. In March 2015, Snapdeal acquired e-commerce management software and fulfilment solution provider, Unicommerce.com (Verma and Dalal, 2015).
10. In March 2015, Snapdeal entered into the financial services marketplace by acquiring a majority stake of Rupee Power which provides a digital platform for financial products to customers (Biswarup Gooptu, 2015).
11. In April 2015, Snapdeal acquired mobile-payments company FreeCharge.com (Thoppil, 2015).
12. In September 2015, Snapdeal acquired Reduce Data, a programmatic display advertising platform (Biswarup Gooptu, 2015).

The company is not profitable, as like other e-commerce companies, it is plagued by issues of security, logistics, and supply chain complexes. It has to be different in its assortments and diversify its products and services as it has quite a number of sellers registered on its site.

Albeit, in a swift turnaround during the financial year 2019-20, the company clocked revenues of ₹ 899 crore, with net loss shrinking to ₹ 188 crore from a staggering ₹ 5,143 crore in 2017. The company claims to have over 27 million unique buyers who purchased from the company in 2020, in comparison to a mere 8.99 million in 2018.

Despite its newfound focus, reclaiming lost territory won't be easy for Snapdeal. In 2015, Snapdeal held over 30 percent of the e-commerce market in India and had even set ambitions to take on Flipkart for the top spot. However, since the near-death experience in 2017, and the eventual resurgence, India's e-commerce industry has seen some serious transformation—following the launch of JioMart, challenging Amazon India and Flipkart.

11.2 Flipkart

Flipkart was established in 2007 by Sachin Bansal and Binny Bansal, both alumni of the Indian Institute of Technology, Delhi. They worked for Amazon.com before quitting their job and founding their own company. It was started with the objective of making books easily available to anyone who had internet access. For the first three years, Flipkart was known as an online books vendor. It wanted to provide the best customer experience, management, bandwidth and capital and infrastructure to expand the business. Only 100 books were sold in 2007 and on December 31, 2007 the company even had a zero order day. By end of 2008, the sales had crossed over a thousand a day and in 2009, the company started getting noticed in the book business.

Off late, it ventured into everything from movies to music, games, mobiles, cameras, computers, healthcare and personal products, home appliances and electronics, stationery, perfumes, toys, apparels and shoes.

Flipkart had a market cap of US$ 11 billion (Business-standard.com, 2014). However, the pertinent point here is that why was Flipkart valued at US$ 11 billion when it hadn't posted any profits yet and how was the valuation done?

When a financial investor like a private equity firm invests in a company, they are not interested in earning a regular income from their investment. They would rather be interested in the return they would get when they sell off their investment. Hence, the valuation of Flipkart was not driven by the revenue or profits it was earning at the point but by the potential earnings in future. Venture capitalists and private equity firms used GMV or gross merchandise value, i.e. the total value of all the goods sold on Flipkart as the principal measure for valuation.

11.2.1 Acquisitions:

1. In 2010, Flipkart acquired WeRead, a social book discovery tool (VCCircle, 2010).
2. In 2011, Flipkart acquired Mime360, a digital content

platform company (Pahwa 2011).

3. In 2012, Flipkart acquired Letsbuy.com, an Indian e-retailer in electronics. Flipkart had bought the company for an estimated US$ 25 million (Business Standard, 2012).
4. In 2014, Flipkart acquired Myntra.com in an estimated ₹ 20 billion deal (Indian Express, May 22, 2014).
5. In 2015, Flipkart acquired Bangalore based global mobile network Adiquity for an undisclosed amount (Vardhan 2015) and also acquired a mobile marketing start-up Appiterate to strengthen its mobile platform (Vardaan, 2015).

Flipkart charges commission from seller who sells their product on Flipkart (10 percent of theproduct price). It offers preferred customer service also on an annual subscription to its user base. In this, preferential service is offered to customers such as they can purchase any deal before 15 minutes of scheduled opening. It charges annual fee from the retailer who lists its products on the website. Also, Flipkart has a logistic service named "Ekart" which provides logistics service not only to Flipkart but to other e-commerce companies as well. Flipkart also acquired Myntra which further boosted its overall revenue.

Flipkart launched its marketplace business model in 2013, transforming from the existing regular inventory model. This was after a probe by the Enforcement Directorate for alleged breach of the Foreign Exchange Management Act for possible violation of foreign investment rules. For every e-commerce company, consumer base is more important and the continuous focus on latest technology such as delivery mechanism, payment mechanism will keep it ahead of its competitors by reducing the acquisition costs. The company failed to get a grip over the digital market as implied by the shutdown of Flipkart's digital music offering service Flyte on June 17, 2013.

Flipkart has been marred by controversy also which dented its reputation also, following the October 6, 2014, "Big Billion

Day" sale, whereby many users could not place any order because of the high server load and errors which led to frustration among customers and those who placed orders got an email saying that their order got cancelled. Most of the products were sold for a price less than the cost price and Flipkart was accused of killing competition which led to the competitors filing complaint against Flipkart to the Commerce Ministry claiming that selling products for less than the cost price was against the commerce policy of the country.

It was embroiled in a controversy again with The Commercial Taxes Department of Kerala issuing a notice to Flipkart in November 2013 seeking details of goods it sold in Kerala and imposed penalties of ₹ 9.49 crore and ₹ 37.65 crore on the company. However, Flipkart filed a petition in High Court questioning the authority of the State Commercial Tax Department in demanding VAT from it and also challenged the penalty imposed on it.

In 2018, Flipkart was in the leading position with 31.9 percent market share as an online retailer in India, while Amazon had a market share of 31.2 percent. Besides, the combined sales from Myntra and Jabong increased Flipkart's market share to 38.3 percent. In August 2018, American retail giant Walmart bought a 77 percent stake in Flipkart for US$ 16 billion, bringing the company's valuation to more than US$ 20 billion.

In 2019, Flipkart released the in-app streaming service "Flipkart Video" to compete with Amazon's premium video streaming service Amazon Prime.

Flipkart's competition with world class global e-commerce giant Amazon has been giving the company a run for its money. Currently, the difference in market share between the two companies is not much. Undoubtedly, Flipkart is ruling the market compared to others in the Indian fashion and lifestyle and budget smartphone segment. Will the company be able to maintain its current position against Amazon in the future, only time will tell?

12

Taxation of E-commerce

Taxation acts as a tool of good governance, allowing economies to grow while helping to improve society as a whole. Electronic commerce and globalization are challenges to traditional tax regimes. Historically, goods were physical, and hence the production, distribution and consumption of these goods was easily taxable. Physical goods were produced at a manufacturing plant, shipped off to wholesalers and boxed on retailers' shelves, with the final consumer walking away with a paid for and taxed product. Tax collection was in the hands of retailers. The retailer charged consumers VAT or sales tax, and then remitted it to the government.

12.1 E-commerce and Commodity Taxation

The development of e-commerce has changed the way businesses operate. It has also challenged the adequacy and fundamental validity of principles of international taxation such as physical presence, place of establishment, etc., that have formed the basis for assessing tax liability.

A commodity that is sold in a bricks and mortar store and, therefore, subject to taxation would be deemed to be different if sold through e-commerce and escapes taxation. Further, those buying through e-commerce are likely to be the more affluent sections of society. This exacerbates inequity.

Furthermore, given its projected phenomenal rate of growth, if e-commerce is not taxed there will be sharp erosion of the tax bases of governments that primarily levy sales taxes. It is well recognized that e-commerce presents some formidable challenges for the tax administration. Both the origin as well as the destination principles of commodity taxation applied at the sub-national level in a country such as

India would find it hard to deal with e-commerce. With the physical location of both the buyer and the seller of the commodity in question irrelevant for the transaction, assigning tax liability would be hard.

In addition, many goods (such as software) sold through e-commerce are directly downloaded and do not necessarily have a physical presence. Given the vast scale of anticipated e-commerce transactions, then, smaller the scale of government, the greater would be the difficulty of taxing e-commerce. The central Government with its reach throughout the country may find it easier to tax e-commerce than individual state governments and local governments. This further centralization of tax authority and the continued need to further decentralize public expenditures would require devolution of larger and larger funds to state governments. This would put greater stress on the structure of fiscal transfers, necessitating a devolution plan that is transparent, fair and acceptable to all levels of government. This development is a further challenge to Indian federalism and requires urgent attention from academics and policy makers.

With the advent of EC, even smaller corporations and individuals can aspire to have a global presence. Correspondingly, EC has also bridged the gap between developed and developing countries. It, has therefore, become extremely essential to provide a legal and tax environment that is conducive to the growth and development of these technologies.

Taxation issues have a bearing on the very foundations and growth potential of any economic idea. In the case of e-commerce, the ramifications are global and affect the very concept and development of e-commerce, as well as the policy that each developing country would need to adopt regarding its foreign trade and internal taxation. This is of importance as for most developing countries, domestic taxes and import and export duties, continue to be the primary source of revenue. On the one hand, the 'digital economy' holds the potential of significant growth and the hope of a significant contribution to fiscal revenues. On the other hand, there is apprehension that a shift to digital commerce may shrink the tax base. Therefore, a fundamental review of tax policies and laws is required as these have their origins in traditional, off-line commerce.

12.2 Theoretical Aspects of Taxing E-commerce

Taxation of any economic transaction requires that it can be legally verified that a transaction between the buyer and the seller has taken place, implying that the administrative procedures needed to generate the required verification are important. Verification can either be direct, for example, through observation of the transaction by a representative of the tax authorities or indirect, for example, through auditing of the parties involved in the transaction. In most cases, direct verification would be prohibitively costly making indirect verification through auditing the commonly used method in modern societies. Since auditing of firms takes place for other reasons thanfor raising tax revenue from commodity taxation, the marginal cost of generating the sufficient information for levying commodity taxes through auditing of firms is negligible.

Auditing of households for tax purposes may be effective in establishing how much income is earned, but ineffective in establishing the consumption levels of specific goods. In some cases, however, verification must take place through registration of the actions of the buyer. To what extent this is practically possible or economically feasible, very much depends on the type of good being traded, in particular whether it is a digitalized or a physical good. In any case, some form of direct verification will be needed.

Since e-commerce transcends national boundaries, it will often be the case that seller and buyer belong to different tax jurisdictions in which case it must be considered which tax principle applies. For commodity taxation, two main inter-tax jurisdictional principles exist: the destination principle and the origin principle. According to the destination principle, it is the destination of the final consumption of the good that determines the size of the tax so that all consumption taking place within the tax jurisdiction is taxed at the same rate. Hence, under the destination principle, exports of goods are untaxed while imports are taxed at the same rate as goods produced and sold domestically.

Under the origin (or the source) principle, it is the origin of the commodity, i.e. the location of the seller, that determines the size of the tax so that all goods produced within the tax jurisdiction are taxed at the same rate irrespective of the final destination of the good. Hence, according to the origin principle, exports are taxed at the same rate as goods produced and sold domestically while imports are untaxed. Of course, for transactions between sellers and buyers belonging to the same tax jurisdiction, the tax liability will be independent of the tax principle.

The choice of tax principle will affect the administrative procedures needed to generate the required verification. Since the tax authorities can only audit entities within their own jurisdiction application of the origin principle, it implies that auditing of firms will generate the required verification. However, when the destination principle applies, the seller will be located outside the jurisdiction of the tax authorities levying the tax and alternative methods for obtaining verification are needed. To describe these methods in detail, it is convenient to treat the cases of digitalized goods and physical goods separately.

12.3 The Case of Digitized Goods

For digitalized goods, the verification of a transaction is particularly difficult due to the anonymity provided by the internet. If the origin principle applies or when the seller and buyer belong to the same tax jurisdiction, verification should be obtained through auditing of the seller. The problem here is that due to digital goods being non-rival goods where the sale of one unit of a digital good (e.g. a computer program) does not reduce the potential for selling the same good to another customer, the same good can be sold unlimited number of times and the problem of the tax authorities becomes one of establishing how many transactions have taken place.

Auditing of the cost side of the selling firm will not yield the required information whereas auditing of the financial transactions of the seller, that is going through all payments made intothe accounts of the seller, could provide the required information. That could prove tobe quite a big task and even though the required verification could be provided but this way the costs to the tax authorities might be very high. In this case, origin taxation of e-commerce in digitized goods will not generate a lot of revenue as firms will expect the tax authorities to be unwilling to devote the resources required for effective auditing.

Under the destination principle, the tax authorities will have to establish verification through information gathered from the buyers. Two options could be possible: either by verifying the transaction through establishing that the digitalized good (computer program, mp3-file etc.) has been transferred onto the computer of the buyer through the internet or by verifying that a payment has taken place e.g., through a credit card payment. Regarding the first option, it could be argued that from a technical point of view, such evidence could be extracted from the computers or the networks involved in the transaction.

Specialist computer forensics firms are capable of establishing the history of a computer even if the user of the computer should attempt to erase any evidence of the transaction having taken place. The relevant observation is, however, that such verification would be extremely costly and given the likely size of the tax burden to be imposed on the transaction through this verification, the costs would be considered prohibitively high. The second option could be viable, provided the tax authorities can get the information needed from the credit card companies.

Hence, transactions involving purely digitized goods should be expected to generate very little tax revenue no matter what tax principle is applied. Thus, e-commerce in digitized goods should for all practical purposes be considered untaxable implying that if e-commerce in digital goods substitutes for trade in commodities that are subject to taxation, the revenue of the tax authorities may be in jeopardy.

12.4 The Case of Physical Goods

Since physical goods either can be sold through the conventional retail trade channel or through the internet, a comparison of the tax aspects for the two types of trade may be informative. A typical aspect of conventional retail trade is that the seller and buyer belong to the same tax jurisdiction, implying that the tax principle employed is unimportant. As it is argued earlier, auditing of firms is much more effective than auditing of households implying that it will be most efficient to obtain the verification needed for tax purposes through auditing of firms. As a practical matter, the seller is usually required to collect the tax on behalf of the tax authorities.

For e-commerce, the seller and the buyer may typically reside in different tax jurisdictions, implying that the choice of tax principle becomes important.

For e-commerce in physical goods under origin taxation, nothing is really different from the case of conventional trade. Of course, an explicit definition of what determines the location of the seller needs to be stated in this case. It could either be the physical location of the server servicing the website of the seller or the physical location of the storage and shipping facilities actually handling the shipments of the goods sold to the final customers.

To make verification of location as easy as possible, it would probably be preferable to use the physical location of the storage and shipping facilities as defining the location of the seller. Just as with ordinary retail trade, auditing of the cost side of firms will be effective in establishing the required verification. Physical goods are rival goods where the sale of one unit of the good prevents the seller from selling the same good to another customer. Hence, effective auditing of the resource use of firms will make it possible for the tax authorities to tax the transaction no matter whether the good is sold through a bricks and mortar retail store or through an internet-based store.

Therefore, it is the effective auditing of firms selling physical goods that make such goods taxable. It does not matter for the taxability how the good is delivered to the buyer e.g., whether the buyer collects it in the store or the good is delivered by a courier. In neither case, representative of the tax authorities is present to verify that the transaction has taken place. Verification is obtained indirectly through effective auditing. Collection of the tax will in both cases be taken care of by the seller.

Use of the destination principle for e-commerce requires that the transaction be verified in relation to the acquisition of the good by the buyer.

The important property of physical goods compared to digitized goods is that they have to be delivered physically to the buyer making the point of delivery an obvious possibility for the verification of transaction. How the verification should take place would depend on whether or not the tax jurisdiction of the buyer has customs control. With an effective customs control, direct verification is possible as the good passes through the customs control. Without customs control, indirect verification is still possible since the physical good has to be handed over to the buyer by a courier.

By auditing the courier firm, the required verification can be established implying that it should be possible to use destination taxation of e-commerce in physical goods. There are, however, some more practical matters that have to be considered mainly with respect to the administrative procedures used to make sure that the right tax liability is levied on and collected from a given transaction.

These administrative procedures are important as they affect the incentives of both firms and households to participate in the e-commerce market. For firms it is important how much of the tax collection (on behalf of "foreign" tax authorities) is required to be involved with since unduly complicated administrative procedures will be considered an additional cost for firms participating in e-commerce. For households, the administrative procedures may affect the degree of uncertainty related to trading with (more or less) anonymous sellers on the internet, and if some procedures increase the perceived level of uncertainty this will discourage households from using e-commerce.

For the administrative procedures for taxation of e-commerce, at least three options are available. They are as under:

1. The selling firm could calculate, collect and forward the tax on a given transaction based on the tax rate prevailing in the tax jurisdiction of the buyer for that kind of commodity. This would create full certainty for the consumer regarding the total price of the good purchased, including tax and shipping costs, at the point in time when the purchase is made. Such a procedure would, on the other hand, impose substantial administrative burdens on firms by effectively requiring them to register with the tax authorities in all the tax jurisdictions (countries) they do trade with.
2. A second possibility be still to have the selling firm calculating the tax but to have the courier handling the shipment of the good collecting the tax revenue from the consumer when the good is delivered. This would still require extensive knowledge on part of the selling firm about the commodity tax systems in "foreign" tax jurisdictions, and also provide the consumer with full information about the total price of the good at the point of sale. The tax collection would be moved entirely into the tax jurisdiction of the buyer but would, of course, impose some handling costs on the courier. Given that the

selling firm still needs extensive knowledge of (many) "foreign" commodity tax systems, it is not obvious that this procedure would be more efficient than when the seller also collects the tax.

For both procedures, it must be considered how likely non-compliance with the tax collection will be, and what can be done to prevent non-compliance. Obviously, the selling firm has no direct economic incentive to become registered with the tax authorities in other tax jurisdictions. Of course, if the tax jurisdiction is a country with customs control, it is possible to exclude non-registered foreign firms by simply stopping any goods passing through the customs control that are not shipped from a registered firm. To what extent this will solve the problem of non-compliance depends on the efficiency of the customs control. Considering the efficiency of these tax collection procedures, the costs of having an effective customs control should be taken into account. When the commodity tax jurisdictions belong to the same country (or a customs union) with no customs control for inter-tax jurisdictional trade, non-compliance may be much harder to prevent. The obvious case here is the US where a requirement of registration with out-of-state tax authorities is likely to be unconstitutional.

3. A third option would be to remove all responsibilities regarding tax calculation and tax collection from the seller and delegate that to the courier firm handling the shipment of the good. For the consumers that would certainly add some uncertainty about the total price of the good at the point of sale. For the courier firms additional handling costs are imposed (which obviously must be passed on to the consumers as higher shipping costs). How to deal with the compliance issue again depends on whether the tax jurisdictions have their own customs control. In case effective customs control is possible, it would be natural to let the customs office calculate the tax payment and just

let the courier collect the tax. Without a customs authority, the tax authorities could induce compliance by performing effective tax auditing of the courier firms.

Which of these procedures should be preferred, all have their pros and cons. Requiring the seller to handle all the tax administration will presumably reduce the number of firms selling through the internet, thereby effectively reducing the degree of competition on that market leading to higher consumer prices. Similarly, letting the courier firms handling the tax administration would lead to increased uncertainty about the final consumer price, leading to reduced demand from (risk averse) consumers. Of course, the selling firms could try to resolve that uncertainty by informing their customers about relevant tax regulations but that advice would be merely informative and not legally binding.

Taking these administrative aspects into account, reveals that although there is nothing formally hindering destination taxation of e-commerce in physical goods, it is not necessarily straightforward to set up proper administrative procedures that will be conducive to a well-functioning e-commerce market. Using the origin principle is somewhat less problematic as tax calculation and tax collection is done within the tax jurisdiction of the seller, and the buyers will enjoy full certainty regarding the tax and shipping included price of the good.

13

E-commerce and Goods and Services Tax (GST)

Restructuring of the tax system has constituted a major component of fiscal reforms initiated since 1991. The main focus of the tax reforms has been on simplification and rationalisation of both direct and indirect taxes with the objective of augmenting revenues and removing anomalies in the tax structure. Tax reforms since 1991 have brought the tax system much closer to international tax practices. Government's concern with tax reforms is reflected in the appointment of a number of committees in recent years to review the tax system.

13.1 Commodity Taxation in India Prior to the Introduction of GST

Prior to the introduction of GST on July 1, 2017, the indirect tax system of India suffered from various disabilities. There was a burden of *tax-on-tax* in the pre-GST system of Central excise duty and the sales tax system of the States. The introduction of Central VAT (CENVAT) did remove the cascading burden of taxes to a good extent by providing a mechanism of set-offs for tax paid on inputs and services up to the stage of production, and was an improvement over the pre-CENVAT Central excise duty. Similarly, the introduction of VAT by the States removed the cascading effect by giving set-off for tax paid on inputs as well as tax paid on previous purchases and again was an improvement over the previous sales tax regime.

However, both the CENVAT and the State VAT had certain deficiencies. CENVAT was deficient because it did not extend to include chain of value additions in the distributive trade below the stage of production. Further, it did not include several Central taxes (such as additional excise duties, additional customs duties, surcharges etc.) in its overall framework. Hence, the benefits of a comprehensive input tax set-offs was not available to manufacturers/dealers under CENVAT.

Likewise, in the State-level VAT scheme, CENVAT load on the goods was not removed and the cascading effect of that part of tax burden had remained unrelieved. Moreover, there were several taxes in the States (such as luxury tax, entertainment tax, etc.) which had not been subsumed under the VAT. In addition, although the burden of Central sales tax (CST) on inter-State movement of goods had been lessened with reduction of CST rate from 4 percent to 2 percent, this burden had also not been fully phased out.

13.2 Introduction of GST: A Historic Tax Reform

After an arduous journey of 12 years—beginning with the mention of Goods and Services Tax (GST) by the then Finance Minister Shri P. Chidambaram in his Budget Speech for 2005-06 on February 28, 2005—GST finally became operative on July 1, 2017. The historic tax reform saw various ups and downs during this period.

13.2.1 What is GST? GST is a tax on goods and services with comprehensive and continuous chain of set-off benefits up to the retailer level. It is essentially a tax only on value addition at each stage, and a supplier at each stage is permitted to set-off, through a tax credit mechanism, the GST paid on the purchase of goods and services. Ultimately, the burden of GST is borne by the end-user (i.e. final consumer) of the commodity/service.

According to clause 12A of Article 366 of the Constitution, *goods and services tax* means any tax on supply of goods, or services or both except taxes on the supply of the alcoholic liquor for human consumption. According to the same Article, *goods* includes all materials, commodities, and articles (clause 12), *services* means anything other than goods (clause 26A) and *State* with reference to Articles 246A, 268,

269, 269A and Article 279A includes a Union Territory with legislature (clause 26B).

The power to levy GST is derived from Article 246A of the Constitution which confers concurrent powers to both Parliament and State Legislatures to make laws with respect to GST. However, clause 2 of Article 246A read with Article 269A provides exclusive power to the Parliament to legislate with respect to inter-state trade or commerce. The taxable event under GST is the supply of goods and/or services. CGST and SGST are levied on intra-state supplies while IGST is levied on inter-state supplies.

GST is a comprehensive indirect tax levy on manufacture, sale and consumption of goods as well as services at the national level. GST is an indirect tax for the whole of India to make it one unified common market. GST is designed to give India a world class tax system and improve tax collections. It would end the long-standing distortions of differential treatment of manufacturing sector and services sector. GST will facilitate seamless credit across the entire supply chain and across all States under a common tax base.

13.2.2 Objectives of GST: The basic objective of tax reforms in any country should be to establish a tax system that is economically efficient, distributionally acceptable, and simple to administer. GST is India's most ambitious and remarkable indirect tax reform. Its objective is to levy a single uniform tax across India on all goods and services. Implementing a new tax, encompassing both goods and services, by the Centre and the States in a large and complex federal system, is perhaps unprecedented in modern global tax history.

Signifying the spirit of co-operative federalism, GST is a historic and game-changing tax reform. Domestically, it will help improve governance, strengthen tax institutions, facilitate *make-in-India* by *making-one-India*, and impart buoyancy to the tax base. The Indian GST is 21st century's global standard for VAT in large federal systems.

As the world economy slows, and increasing financial

volatility and turbulence become the *newest normal*, only a few economies have the resilience to be a refuge of stability and the potential to be an outpost of opportunity. India is one of those few. As oil and commodity prices continue to be soft, macroeconomic stability seems reasonably assured for India. This bedrock of stability coupled with reforms can propel the economy to a high growth trajectory. Key amongst these reforms is the national level GST.

Implementation of GST leaves behind an inefficient, complicated and fragmented indirect tax system. Switch over to GST is fraught with many problems—administrative and technical. However, such problems are endemic of any change of revolutionary proportions. Many of the problems will be transitory in nature. No one should expect a foolproof GST from day one. GST Council has successfully sorted out political, administrative and implementation differences among the stakeholders and it is competent enough to grapple with any future challenges and rectifications

GST requires a very high level of compliance. The age of hand-written ledgers, account books, balance sheets and manual record-keeping is gone. Everything will now be online and need to be updated regularly.

Since major Central and State indirect taxes have got subsumed under GST, the multiplicity of taxes has been substantially reduced which, in turn, would decrease the operating costs of the country's tax system. With GST in place, the burden of Central sales tax (CST) has also been removed. The uniformity in tax rates and procedures across the country will go a long way in reducing compliance costs.

13.2.3 Salient Features of GST: GST has subsumed a profusion of Central and State indirect taxes to create a single unified market. GST will make India a seamless national market, boosting trade and industry and hence growth rate.

As against the erstwhile system of tax on the manufacture of goods or on sale of goods or on provision of services, GST is applicable on *supply* of goods or services or both.

A. Destination-based Consumption Tax: GST is a destination-based consumption tax as against the erstwhile origin-based tax system. This implies that all SGST collected will ordinarily accrue to the State where the consumer of the goods and/or services sold resides. In other words, the tax would accrue to the taxing authority which has jurisdiction over the place of consumption which is also termed as place of supply.

In the case of inter-State trade, the inter-State seller pays IGST on the sale of his goods to the Central Government after adjusting credit of IGST, CGST and SGST on his purchases (in that order). The exporting State transfers to the Centre the credit of SGST used in payment of IGST. The importing dealer claims credit of IGST while discharging his output tax liability (both CGST and SGST) in his own State. The Centre transfers to the importing State the credit of IGST used in payment of SGST. Since GST is a destination-based tax, all SGST on the final product ordinarily accrues to the consuming State.

B. Dual GST Model: It is a dual GST with the Centre and the States simultaneously levying it on a common base. GST levied by the Centre on intra-State supply of goods and services is called Central GST (CGST) and that levied by the States (including Union territories with legislature) is called State GST (SGST). Union territories without legislature levy Union Territory GST (UT-GST).

CGST and SGST are levied simultaneously on every transaction of supply of goods and services. Further, both CGST and SGST are levied on the same price or value unlike the erstwhile State VAT which was levied on the value of the goods inclusive of Central Value Added Tax (CENVAT).

While the location of the supplier and the recipient within the country is immaterial for the purpose of CGST, SGST is chargeable only when the supplier and the recipient are both located within the same State.

This dual GST model is implemented through multiple statutes (one for CGST and one each SGST statute for every State). To the extent feasible, uniform procedures for collection of both CGST and SGST are prescribed in the respective legislations for CGST and SGST. The basic features of law such as chargeability, definition of taxable event and taxable person, measure of levy including valuation provisions, basis of classification etc. are uniform across these statutes as far as practicable.

CGST and SGST are paid electronically into the accounts of the Centre and the States separately. Centre levies and administers CGST and IGST while respective States levy and administer SGST.

C. Integrated GST (IGST) on Inter-State Transactions and Imports: IGST mechanism has been designed to ensure seamless flow of input tax credit from one State to another. Centre levies IGST which is CGST plus SGST on all inter-State transactions of taxable goods and services.

D. Input Tax Credit (ITC): According to Section 16(1) of the Central Goods and Services Tax Act, 2017, "Every registered person shall, subject to such conditions and restrictions as may be prescribed and in the manner specified in Section 49, be entitled to take credit of input tax charged on any supply of goods or services or both to him which are used or intended to be used in the course or furtherance of his business and the said amount shall be credited to the electronic credit ledger of such person".

ITC is an important feature of GST. There are well-defined rules for availing ITC.

E. GST and Foreign Trade: Exports are zero-rated supplies under GST law. Supplies made to SEZs are zero-rated and considered as physical exports. As per explanation to clause (1) of Article 269A of the Constitution, IGST (CGST plus SGST) will be levied on all imports into the territory of India. Thus, import of goods is treated as inter-state supplies and hence subject to IGST in addition to the applicable customs duties. Import of services is treated as inter-state supplies and hence subject to IGST.

13.3 Electronic Commerce, Electronic Commerce Operators and GST

Electronic commerce means the supply of goods or services or both, including digital products over digital or electronic network [Section 2(44) of the CGST Act, 2017]. Electronic commerce operator means any person who owns, operates or manages digital or electronic facility or platform for electronic commerce [Section 2(45) of the CGST Act, 2017].

As per Section 9(5) of the CGST Act, 2017, "The Government may, on the recommendations of the Council, by notification, specify categories of services the tax on intra-State supplies of which shall be paid by the electronic commerce operator if such services are supplied through it, and all the provisions of this Act shall apply to such electronic commerce operator as if he is the supplier liable for paying the tax in relation to the supply of such services:

Provided that where an electronic commerce operator does not have a physical presence in the taxable territory, any person representing such electronic commerce operator for any purpose in the taxable territory shall be liable to pay tax:

Provided further that where an electronic commerce operator does not have a physical presence in the taxable territory and also he does not have a representative in the said territory, such electronic commerce operator shall appoint a person in the taxable territory for the purpose of paying tax and such person shall be liable to pay tax".

It may be recalled that during pre-GST era supplying goods through e-commerce platform was not well-defined. E-commerce operators (like Amazon and Flipkart) were treated as facilitators by some states (like West Bengal and Kerala) and hence not required to register themselves for VAT. Contrarily, in some states (e.g. Uttar Pradesh) they were required to file a VAT declaration and other documents. Due to differential practices of states in this regard, there was lot of confusion and ambiguity. Under GST, there are clear-cut provisions applicable to e-commerce sector on all-India basis.

There is no complication regarding inter-state movement of goods.

13.3.1 Tax Collection at Source (TCS): TCS means that any dealer selling through e-commerce will receive payment after deduction of tax at specified rate. Since TCS is mainly for e-commerce aggregators, it is necessary to understand what is e-commerce and who is an electronic commerce operator.

13.3.2 Legal Provisions for TCS: With regard to tax collection at source (TCS), sub-sections (1) and (3) of Section 52 of CGST Act, 2017 read as follows,

"(1) Notwithstanding anything to the contrary contained in this Act, every electronic commerce operator (hereafter in this section referred to as the "operator"), not being an agent, shall collect an amount calculated at such rate not exceeding one percent, as may be notified by the Government on the recommendations of the Council, of the net value of taxable supplies made through it by other suppliers where the consideration with respect to such supplies is to be collected by the operator...(3) The amount collected under sub-section (1) shall be paid to the Government by the operator within ten days after the end of the month in which such collection is made, in such manner as may be prescribed".

Benefit of threshold exemption is not available to e-commerce operators and they are liable to be registered irrespective of the value of supply made by them. Thus, Amazon is e-commerce operator because it is facilitating actual suppliers to supply goods through its platform.

If a person is supplying own products through his own hosting website then tax collection at source (TCS) will not take place because TCS is required when taxable supply is made through e-commerce operator by other supplier and consideration is collected by e-commerce operator. When someone is selling own product through own website there is no need for TCS. Here normal GST rate will be applicable.

If someone is purchasing goods from different vendors and selling such goods on his own website under his own billing, then TCS is not needed because supply is not made by other supplier. Again, Amazon is e-commerce operator because it is facilitating suppliers to supply goods through its platform (popularly called market place model or fulfilment model). However, Amazon will not be treated as e-commerce operators in relation to those supplies which it makes on its own account (popularly called inventory model).

Twenty-sixth Meeting of the GST Council held on March 10, 2018 decided to postpone the applicability of TCS until June 30, 2018. Provisions relating to TCS were again deferred for another 3 months till September-end, 2018.

On September 13, 2018, Government notified the provision part of Section 52 of the CGST Act, 2017 which had been kept in abeyance since the rollout of GST on July 1, 2017. As per the notification, TCS provisions under GST regime took effect from October 1, 2018. Rate of TCS for intra-state supplies is 1 percent of net taxable supplies (0.5 percent CGST plus 0.5 percent SGST). Rate of TCS for inter-state supplies (IGST) is 1 percent of net taxable supplies.

Thus, e-commerce firms have to collect tax at the specified rate before making the payment to the supplier for proceeds of sale. E-commerce operators had opposed TCS arguing that it would add to their compliance burden due to the cumbersome reporting provisions. E-commerce firms have to furnish a monthly statement and an annual statement containing details of the outward supplies. In addition, they have to deposit tax collected at source by 10th of the next month in which the tax was collected.

With the TCS provisions coming into force, tax authorities are empowered to monitor e-commerce transactions and ensure that suppliers selling their goods through e-commerce platforms do not get away with under-reporting their turnover.

TCS implementation as a tool to check tax evasion comes at a time when GST revenues are lagging behind budgeted targets and the tax authorities are struggling to stabilize revenues at higher level. Government is hoping that TCS along with e-way bill implementation will prevent non-reporting and under-reporting of transactions thereby enlarging the taxpayer base.

13.4 Components of GST

The introduction of GST on July 1, 2017 was a significant reform in the field of indirect taxes in India. Multiple taxes levied on goods and services by the Centre and the States were replaced by GST.

A dual GST model is in place in view of the federal structure of India. Centre and the States now simultaneously levy GST on every supply of goods or services or both which takes place within a State or Union Territory (i.e. intra-state trade). Hence, there are three components of GST so far as intra-state trade is concerned.

- Central Goods and Services Tax (CGST).
- State Goods and Services Tax (SGST).
- Union Territory Goods and Services Tax (UT-GST).

Another important component of GST is Integrated Goods and Service Tax (IGST) which is levied by the Centre on inter-state supply of goods or services or both. IGST rate is broadly equal to CGST rate plus SGST rate. SGST component of IGST accrues to the consumer state.

Similarly, a compensation cess on certain specified goods is imposed to compensate States for any revenue loss on account of implementation of GST.

13.4.1 Central Goods and Services Tax (CGST): GST levied by the Centre on intra-State supply of goods or services or both is called CGST. It is levied under Central Goods and Services Tax (CGST) Act, 2017 which makes provisions for the levy and collection of tax on intra-state supply of goods or services or both by the Central Government. The Act is divided into 21 chapters which deal with matters connected with the levy, collection and administration of GST.

13.4.2 State Goods and Services Tax (SGST): GST levied by the States on intra-state supply of goods or services or both under their respective SGST Acts is called SGST. Union territories with legislature (Delhi, Puducherry and Jammu and Kashmir) are covered under the definition of *state*. However, Union territories without legislature are governed by Union Territory Goods and Services Tax (UT-GST), Act, 2017.

The Secretariat of the GST Council released the Model GST Law (MGL) in November 2016. The MGL provided a common draft of Central GST (CGST) Act and State GST (SGST) Act. MGL also included the draft of Integrated GST (IGST) Act as well as draft GST Valuation Rules.

Telangana was the first State to pass the SGST Act. Jammu and Kashmir was the last to do so and that too post-GST implementation.

13.4.3 Union Territory Goods and Services Tax (UT-GST): Union Territories without legislature are governed by a separate Act, namely the Union Territory Goods and Services Tax (UT-GST), Act, 2017 which makes provisions for the levy and collection of tax on intra-UT supply of goods or services or both in the Union Territories without legislature. Thus, it extends to the following five Union Territories:

1. Andaman and Nicobar Islands.
2. Lakshadweep.
3. Dadra and Nagar Haveli and Daman and Diu.
4. Chandigarh.
5. Ladakh.

Why was there the need for a separate Act for UTs without legislature? It is notable that the Constitution (One Hundred and First Amendment) Act, 2016 inserted a new clause, viz. clause 26B in Article 366 of the Constitution. As per this clause, *State* with reference to Articles 246A, 268, 269, 269A and 279A includes a Union Territory with legislature. Delhi and Puducherry are Union Territories with legislature and hence covered under the definition of *State* for the purpose of GST.

Unlike States and Union Territories with legislature, Union Territories without legislature do not have their legislative assemblies. Hence, they do not have power to make Acts and Rules. As far as CGST is concerned, it applies to these territories also. However, a separate law, corresponding to SGST, was required for Union Territories without legislatures. Hence, the Central Government passed the Union Territory Goods and Services Tax (UT-GST), Act, 2017.

It is noteworthy in the above context that as per Article 246(4) of the Constitution, the Parliament has powers to make laws with respect to any matter for any part of the territory of India, which is not included in the State, including the matters enumerated in State List (List II) of the Seventh Schedule to the Constitution of India. Therefore, with the approval from the GST Council, the Central Government passed the UT-GST law in the Parliament.

Supply of goods/services within these Union Territories (for example supply by a trader from Chandigarh to another trader in Chandigarh) is subject to CGST plus UT-GST. For the purpose of GST, each of these territories is considered as a separate Union Territory. Thus, if a trader in Andaman and Nicobar Islands supplies goods to a trader in Lakshadweep, it will be treated as inter-state supply and hence subject to IGST.

13.4.4 Integrated Goods and Service Tax (IGST): IGST is levied by the Centre on inter-state supply of goods or services or both. IGST is a mechanism to monitor the inter-state supply of goods or services or both. It is levied by the Central Government on all inter-state transactions of taxable goods and services. IGST rate is broadly equal to CGST rate plus SGST rate. SGST component of IGST accrues to the consumer state. IGST maintains the integrity of input tax credit (ITC) chain in inter-state supplies.

GST makes distinction between intra-state and inter-state supply of goods and services. Hence, IGST—as a part of GST regime—is levied on inter-State supply (including stock transfers) of goods and services. It is levied and collected by the Centre so that the credit chain is not disrupted. IGST also applies on imports.

A. Advantages of IGST Model: The major advantages of IGST model are as under:

1. Maintenance of uninterrupted input tax credit (ITC) chain on inter-State transactions.
2. No upfront payment of tax or substantial blockage of funds for the inter-State seller or buyer.
3. No refund claim in exporting State, as ITC is used up while paying the tax.
4. Self-monitoring mechanism.
5. Level of computerization is limited to inter-State dealers and Central and State Governments are able to computerize their processes expeditiously.
6. As all inter-State dealers are e-registered and correspondence with them is by email, the compliance level is substantially high.
7. IGST can take into account *business-to-business* as well as *business-to-consumer* transactions.
8. It facilitates the seamless flow of ITC across states as it is a destination-based tax, i.e., the IGST amount will be apportioned between the Centre and States although the power to levy and collect IGST lies with the Centre to ensure that a single coordinating agency administers it.

It is noteworthy that CGST, IGST and UT-GST laws are the exclusive domain of the Centre. Central Board of Indirect Taxes and Customs (CBIC)—formerly Central Board of Excise and Customs (CBEC)—is responsible for administration of the CGST, IGST and UT-GST laws. In addition, excise duty regime continues to be administered by the CBIC for levy and collection of Central excise duty on five specified petroleum products as well as on tobacco products. CBIC also continues to handle the work relating to levy and collection of customs duties.

SGST is administered by the respective State Governments through their commercial tax departments

13.5 Rationale for Different Categories of GST

What is the logic for CGST, SGST, UT-GST and IGST? India is a federal polity where both the Centre and the States have been assigned the powers to levy and collect taxes. Both the levels of Government have distinct responsibilities to perform, as per the Constitution, for which they need to raise resources. Therefore, a dual GST is in keeping with the constitutional requirement of fiscal federalism. The Centre and States simultaneously levy GST.

In the pre-GST era, taxation powers between the Centre and the States were clearly demarcated in the constitution with no overlap between the respective domains. In other words, there were no concurrent powers of taxation (or joint occupancy of tax fields) by the two levels of government. Introduction of GST has concurrently empowered the Centre and the States to levy and collect it.

To sum up, GST is meant to evolve an efficient and harmonized consumption-based tax system in the country. GST is a consumption-based tax because the tax is received by the State in which the goods or services are consumed and not by the state in which such goods are manufactured. GST has replaced parallel systems of indirect taxation at the Central and State levels. The changeover to GST is a game-changing tax reform which will significantly contribute to the buoyancy of tax revenues, acceleration of growth, and generation of many positive externalities. Different components of GST are meant to ensure:

- One-country, one-tax and one-market.
- Adequate revenue for both the Centre and the States.

14

GST in Select Countries of the World

GST has claimed world-wide attention as more and more countries are adopting it in varying degrees to reform their systems of commodity taxation.

14.1 Canada

GST was introduced in Canada on January 1, 1991. It replaced a hidden 13.5 percent manufacturers' sales tax (MST) because the MST was hindering the manufacturing sector's ability to export competitively. The introduction of the GST was very controversial. The GST rate is 5 percent, effective January 1, 2008.

GST is levied on supplies of goods and services purchased in Canada and include most products, except certain politically sensitive essentials such as groceries, residential rent, and medical services, and services such as financial services. Businesses which purchase goods and services that are consumed, used or supplied in the course of their *commercial activities* can claim *input tax credits* subject to prescribed documentation requirements. This avoids *cascading*, i.e. the application of the GST on the same good or service several times as it passes from business-to-business on its way to the final consumer. In this way, the tax is essentially borne by the final consumer. This system is not completely effective because dishonest business entities defraud the tax authorities by claiming GST input credits for non-existent sales by a fictional company. Exported goods are exempt (zero-rated), while individuals with low incomes can receive a GST rebate calculated in conjunction with their income tax.

In 1997, the provinces of Nova Scotia, New Brunswick and Newfoundland (now Newfoundland and Labrador) and the

Government of Canada merged their respective sales taxes into the harmonized sales tax (HST). In New Brunswick, and Newfoundland and Labrador, the current HST rate is 13 percent, while in Nova Scotia it was raised from 13 percent to 15 percent, effective July 1, 2010. HST is administered by the Canada Revenue Agency, with revenues divided among participating governments according to an agreed formula. Ontario and British Columbia both harmonized the GST with their provincial sales tax (PST) effective July 1, 2010.

The three territories of Canada (Yukon, Northwest Territories and Nunavut) do not have territorial sales taxes. The government of Quebec administers both the federal GST and the provincial Quebec Sales Tax (QST). It is the only province to administer the federal tax.

The tax is imposed at the rate of 5 percent on the supply of goods and services that are purchased in Canada, except certain items that are either *exempt* or *zero-rated.*

Suppliers who make exempt supplies are not entitled to recover GST paid on inputs acquired for the purposes of making the exempt goods and services. Tax-exempt items include basic groceries, prescription drugs, inward/outbound transportation and medical devices, long-term residential rents, health and dental care, educational services, day-care services, music lessons, legal aid services, and financial services. Certain exports of goods and services are also zero-rated.

14.2 Australia

Australia is the most recent example of an industrialized country replacing a tax at the manufacturing or wholesale level by the GST extending to the retail level. The previous tax was found to be unworkable, in spite of the high degree of sophistication in administration in Australia. It simply could not deal with the variety of supply chain arrangements in a satisfactory manner.

GST in Australia is a value added tax of 10 percent on the sales of most goods and services. GST is levied on most transactions in the production process, but is refunded to all parties in the chain of production other than the final consumer.

The tax was introduced on July 1, 2000, replacing the previous federal wholesale sales tax system and designed to phase out a number of State and Territory Government taxes, duties and levies such as banking taxes and stamp duty.

All Australian businesses whose turnover is above the minimum threshold are required to register for GST. Businesses whose turnover is below the threshold may register if they wish to.

A GST-registered business must charge its customers GST on taxable goods and services it provides, but is entitled to a credit for any GST it has paid for its expenditures on these goods and services as well as capital purchases (called input tax credits). A registered business must periodically lodge business activity statements (monthly, quarterly or annually), and at the same time pay the net amount of GST owed to the tax office. If more GST is paid than collected, a refund is paid by the tax office instead.

Some goods and services (notably salaries, wages, fresh food, and real estate) are exempt from GST. Other goods and services (rental income and financial services) are *input-taxed*, which means that GST is not charged on the sale, but GST paid by that part of the business is not eligible to be claimed as an input tax credit.

GST is applicable to a supply of goods, services and transactions related to real property, obligations or rights. The supply must be for consideration to a relevant entity registered for GST in the course of enterprise. This does not include employment or hobby income.

Certain types of supplies are free of GST as, for example, fresh unprocessed food, medical services, education courses, childcare, pre-owned real estate and exports. When an enterprise purchases goods or services to be consumed or used for re-supply to an end customer they may receive a refund (input tax credit) on the amount of GST contained in the price, which means in effect no GST is paid on those supplies.

New residential and commercial properties are subject to GST but re-sale of existing properties is not. All real estate agent fees on either new or second-hand property are subject to GST. Processed foods such as biscuits, soft drinks, restaurant meals and take-away foods are also subject to GST.

Registered enterprises for GST must complete a business activity statement (BAS) for reporting to the Australian Taxation Office (ATO) for each quarter ending March, June, September and December. Businesses must lodge their Statements with the ATO within twenty working days of the end of each quarter.

Critics have argued that the GST is a regressive tax, which has a more pronounced effect on lower income earners, meaning that the tax consumes a higher proportion of their income, compared to those earning large incomes. However, due to the corresponding reductions in personal income taxes, state banking taxes, federal wholesale taxes and some fuel taxes that were implemented when the GST was introduced, it is claimed by some that people were effectively paying no extra tax.

14.3 Malaysia

GST is a value added tax in Malaysia. GST is levied on most transactions in the production process, but is refunded with the exception of *blocked input tax*, to all parties in the chain of production other than the final consumer.

The existing standard rate for GST effective from April 1, 2015 is 6 percent.

GST was scheduled to be implemented by the government during the third quarter of 2011, but the implementation was delayed until April 1, 2015. Its purpose is to replace the sales-and-service tax which has been used in the country for several decades. The government is seeking additional revenues to offset its budget deficit and reduce its dependence on revenue from Petronas, Malaysia's state-owned oil company. The 6 percent tax replaced a sales-and-service tax of between 5-15 percent.

The Goods and Services Tax Bill, 2009 was tabled for its first reading at the Dewan Rakyat (lower house of the Malaysian Parliament) on December 16, 2009. It was delayed amid mounting criticism. The government responded by asserting that the tax on oil income will not be sustainable in the future.

During the government reading of the 2014 budget, Malaysian Prime Minister Najib Razak announced a GST tax of 6 percent starting on April 1, 2015. Implementing GST tax is a part of the Government's tax reform programme to enhance the capability, effectiveness and transparency of tax administration and management.

During the unveiling of the national budget, it was announced that the following goods and services would be exempted from GST:

1. Agricultural products—paddy, fresh or chilled vegetables, certain provisionally preserved vegetables.
2. Essential foodstuff—oils, salt, flour etc.
3. Livestocks and livestock supplies or poultry—live animals and unprocessed meat.
4. Eggs.
5. Fish—live, fresh, frozen and dried.
6. First 300 kWh of electricity for domestic use.
7. Water for domestic users.
8. Goods supplied to designated areas from Malaysia—Labuan, Langkawi and Tioman.
9. Exported goods.
10. Exported services—such as architecture services in connection with land outside Malaysia.
11. Selected services in Malaysia—such as pilotage, salvage or towage services.
12. International services—such as transport of passengers or goods from a place in Malaysia to a place outside Malaysia.

13. Petrol, diesel and LPG.
14. Sale of residential property.
15. Services provided by government which are not considered commercial services, such as permits, licences etc. Services considered commercial are TV advertisement, rental of equipments, rental of multifunction halls etc.

14.4 New Zealand

GST is a value added tax in New Zealand. GST in New Zealand is designed to be a broad-based system with few exemptions. Exceptions that do exist include rents collected on residential rental properties, donations, precious metals and financial services. End-users pay this tax on all liable goods and services indirectly, in that the purchase price of goods and services includes GST.

The existing rate for GST effective from October 1, 2010 is 15 percent.

GST was introduced by the Fourth Labour Government of New Zealand on October 1, 1986 at a rate of 10 percent on most goods and services. It replaced existing sales taxes for some goods and services. GST was a part of the economic reforms initiated by Labour Finance Minister Roger Douglas. GST was introduced in conjunction with compensating changes to personal income tax rates.

Since its introduction it has had two increases: on July 1, 1989 the rate was increased to 12.5 percent and on October 1, 2010 it was increased again to 15 percent.

GST-registered organisations and individuals pay GST only on the difference between GST-liable sales and GST-liable supplies (i.e. they pay GST on the difference between what they sell and what they buy: income less expenditure). This is accomplished by reconciling GST received (through sales) and GST paid (through purchases) at regular periods (typically every two months, with some qualifying companies opting for one-month or six-month periods), then either paying the difference to the Inland Revenue (IR) if the GST collected on sales is higher or receiving a refund from IR if the GST paid on purchases is higher.

Businesses exporting goods and services from New Zealand are entitled to zero-rate their products: effectively, they charge GST at 0 percent. This permits the business to claim back the input GST, but the eventual, non-New Zealand based consumer does not pay the tax (businesses that produce GST-exempt supplies are not able to claim back input GST).

Because businesses claim back their input GST, the GST inclusive price is usually irrelevant for business purchasing decisions, other than in relation to cash flow issues. Consequently, wholesalers often state prices exclusive of GST, but must collect the full, GST-inclusive price when they make the sale and account to the IR for the GST so collected.

14.5 Singapore

GST in Singapore is a broad-based value added tax levied on import of goods, as well as nearly all supplies of goods and services. The only exemptions are for the sales and leases of residential properties and most financial services. Export of goods and international services are zero-rated.

Before 1986, Singapore's corporate income tax rate and top marginal personal income tax rate both stood at 40 percent. Such high rates were deemed to be uncompetitive. On the recommendation of the 1986 Economic Committee, Singapore's government decided that it needed to shift from direct to indirect taxes, to maintain its international competitiveness in attracting investments, and to sustain its economic growth to create well-paying jobs for Singaporeans.

GST was part of a larger tax restructuring exercise to enable Singapore to shift its reliance from direct taxes to indirect taxes. The government argued that tax reform was necessary to maintain Singapore's competitiveness, to sustain long-term growth and job creation. The government also argued that with an ageing population, Singapore's income tax base was expected to decline. With a broad-based GST, the taxation burden would be more evenly spread among the population.

GST was implemented at a single rate of 3 percent on April 1, 1994, with an assurance that it would not be raised for at least 5 years. To cushion the impact of GST on Singaporean households, an offset package was also introduced. Simultaneously, corporate tax rate and the top marginal personal income tax rate were reduced by 3 percent each. The initial GST rate of 3 percent was among the lowest in the world, as the focus was not to generate substantial revenue, but to allow people to get adjusted to the tax.

In 2002, the Economic Review Committee reviewed Singapore's tax policy, and recommended that further tax reforms were necessary to bring in new investments. The Committee noted that other countries were aggressively reducing their direct tax rates to attract internationally mobile capital and labour, and recommended that the government rely more on GST for its tax revenues, while again cushioning the impact on Singaporean households through an offset package.

Government accepted the Committee's recommendations. The GST rate was increased from 3 percent to 4 percent in 2003, and to 5 percent in 2004. Each increase was accompanied by an offset package that was designed to make the average Singaporean household better off, even after accounting for the additional costs imposed by the increase in GST rates. Direct tax rates were also reduced correspondingly.

On February 15, 2007, Finance Minister Tharman Shanmugaratnam announced that the GST rate would be increased to 7 percent with effect from July 1, 2007.

To maintain the progressive nature of total taxes and transfers on individuals, Singapore reduced income tax on lower-income earners, as well as instituted direct transfer payments to lower-income groups, resulting in an overall lower tax burden for most Singaporean households. These offsets included lower income taxes, lower property taxes, rebates on rental, service and conservancy charges for public housing, and additional subsidies for health, education and community services.

The Singapore government has argued that the GST on its own is a flat tax, but that it is part of an overall fiscal system that is highly progressive: higher-income earners pay the highest fraction of their income in taxes, and also spend more. When all taxes were taken into account (income tax, property tax, GST and other indirect taxes), the top 10 percent of households accounted for 38 percent of the taxes paid, while the top 20 percent contributed 53 percent of all taxes. In contrast, lower-income earners receive substantially more transfers than the taxes they pay. Low- and middle-income households effectively pay *negative* tax.

Some critics contend that basic essentials such as food and healthcare should be made exempt from GST, to help lower-income households. The government argued that having such exemptions would actually help the higher-income more than poorer Singaporeans, because well-off households usually spend much more on essentials (whether food or healthcare or other basic necessities) than a lower-income household. In addition, lower-income households would not benefit much from such an exemption, as spending on essentials constitutes a small proportion of expenditure of lower-income households.

If essentials were to be exempted from GST, there would be a need to make up for the revenue shortfall through a higher GST rate on other goods and services, which lower-income households would also have to bear. The government argued that the experience of other countries demonstrated that granting exemptions would distort production and consumption decisions and cause a contentious and highly complex process of determining the goods and services that merit exemption. This would increase compliance and administration costs for businesses, and these costs would be passed on to consumers.

In addition, the experience of other countries have shown that exempting or reducing GST on certain items did not mean that tax savings would be passed on to consumers. Therefore, the GST should be kept broad-based to keep the GST low and the GST system simple, while help is directly provided to the lower-income groups through transfers and subsidies.

15

Conclusions

The high growth rate of service sector had provided the opportunity to Government to bring under the tax net uncovered services. Due to its high buoyancy, it can provide tremendous revenue to the Government, hence from July, 1994, service tax was introduced on certain services, but slowly more and more services were brought into tax net and now it is imposed on every service except those on negative list. The imposition of service tax was necessary as it will provide fair system of taxation, as there is no point to differentiate between consumption of goods and consumption of services. Service tax is a tax levied by the government on service providers on service transactions, but is actually borne by the customers. The imposition of service tax had led to an increase in the prices of final services used by consumers since it is an indirect tax and works as a prime cost for industry, hence inflationary. Further, as service sector is expanding with time, the share of gross surplus will rise and would lead to an increase in the size of the black economy. Further, there are difficulties in taxing services, as most of the services are in unorganized sector.

With rise in the services, there was a tremendous rise in e-commerce, but this rise in e-commerce had brought in new challenges for the Government of how to tax internet activities, due to problems of location, issue of service provider or seller and the major problem is in taxing digital goods and services. The existing rules of taxation of goods and services in India are not able to solve the problem. Although, e-commerce's growth is in tier-1 or tier-2 cities, the consumer base is low but still it is affecting the tax revenue of state governments, one cannot say the decrease in tax revenue in quantitative terms, as no data is available for e-commerce transactions. However, Bruce and Fox (2000) had estimated losses from e-commerce transactions in US, but estimations were made for year 2006 and 2011, but for year 2011, it raises question as economic crisis started in 2007.

15.1 Growth of Services Sector

Services sector is the fastest growing sector in India, contributing significantly to the GDP. However, in services sector there had been artificial increase in output due to increase in prices of services such as health and education due to privatisation of these services, unpaid work being replaced by paid worker in the market, production resulting in environmental degradation or destruction and increase in waste. Further, it leads to double counting of output and hence over-estimation of GDP.

Most of the activities in the services sector are in the large unorganised sector and due to low literacy rate in the country and poor quality of education, the workers in the unorganised sector have low skills and low productivity. Further, due to technological advancement and services sector being capital intensive, had generated low employment in the sector and most of the population is in the unorganised sector.

The Indian economy had not followed the classical model of stages of development and had skipped the stage of development in which the secondary sector should be dominant unlike tertiary sector. Actually, India is still in colonial mode and copy Western countries, hence borrowed the modern technology from West and since service sector is capital intensive, service sector had grown faster than other sectors. In computer services (software), a large part of the export is the supply of cheap labour and India has yet to develop and export high end IT products.

There are disparities in access of services and a major proportion of the poor in India do not have access to basic services such as health and education. Widespread poverty and accelerated population growth are major constraints, thereby depriving several people of access to basic health and education. The quality of services provided are low due to inadequate infrastructure available not only in rural areas but also in the urban areas as major cities face problems due to power cuts, bumpy roads, traffic congestion and pollution.

In brief, poor infrastructural facilities, non-uniformity in the quality and standard of education, bureaucratic inertia, widespread corruption and unemployable educated youth are the problems in the service sector and its contribution to inclusive growth. The growth in output witnessed in the service sector in recent times is mainly from IT and IT-enabled services while other services that serve as crucial input to working of the Indian economy (as support for agriculture and industry) have not developed as fast as expected. Therefore, recognizing the need for greater penetration of IT services domestically, India has been preparing itself for knowledge-based transformation.

15.2 Taxation of Services

Since GDP is moving in favour of the services sector, its shares is increasing, but services were not taxed therefore that meant tax collection could not rise as much as it could have risen. Tax was not imposed on the growing chunk, such as excise tax on goods, customs on importation, sales tax on sales of goods and on the services component, there was no tax. Till 1994, it was lacunae that while goods were being taxed and services were not taxed, the services sector was growing. Therefore, to increase the collection of indirect tax, more and more burden was falling on excise and customs, and to generate more revenue, tax rate on excise, customs and sales was increasing and therefore it was decided to tax services.

Since, valuation of services is difficult, so one doesn't know what would be the value of a doctor, a chartered accountant or of any other professional services. Therefore, how to value services became a problem as far as levying of the service tax was concerned. Further, indirect taxes are stagflationary and therefore collecting more indirect taxes tends to give more stagflationary component in the economy, therefore, it kept the rate of growth low of what it could be and kept the rate of inflation higher than what it could be. Because the valuation of services is difficult, there is a lot of black economy concentrated in the service sector and hence, taxation is a problem. That is why the service sector is the most underestimated one and also the one in which taxation is not collected.

15.3 Growth of E-commerce

With India's population nearly four times that of the United States and nearly three-fourths of this population living in rural regions, the reach of the internet can provide goods and services which are not available outside the urban areas. India is weakest in the level of internet infrastructure which had held back its growth in internet user base.

Network Readiness Index, 2016, which was released by World Economic Forum (WEF), measures countries success in creating the conditions necessary for a transition to a digitised economy and society. In this index, under different parameters, such as infrastructure, skills, individual usage, business and innovation environment, India has faired poorly. This clearly shows that a strong divide exists between metropolitan cities and remote rural areas. We are not digital ready that is why it is difficult to penetrate into rural areas. Here comes the differentiation with other countries, mainly China, which had shown a tremendous growth in e-commerce so much so that it has surpassed US.

15.4 Taxation of E-commerce

Prior to the introduction of GST on July 1, 2017, the indirect tax system of India suffered from various disabilities. There was a burden of *tax-on-tax* in the pre-GST system of Central excise duty and the sales tax system of the States.

GST is a tax on goods and services with comprehensive and continuous chain of set-off benefits up to the retailer level. It is essentially a tax only on value addition at each stage, and a supplier at each stage is permitted to set-off, through a tax credit mechanism, the GST paid on the purchase of goods and services. Ultimately, the burden of GST is borne by the end-user (i.e. final consumer) of the commodity/service.

Electronic commerce means the supply of goods or services or both, including digital products over digital or electronic network [Section 2(44) of the CGST Act, 2017]. Electronic commerce operator means any person who owns, operates or manages digital or electronic facility or platform for electronic commerce [Section 2(45) of the CGST Act, 2017].

Presently, tax collection at source (TCS) means that any dealer selling through e-commerce will receive payment after deduction of tax at specified rate.

15.5 Lessons from China

India can learn lessons from China so that India's i nternet economy is a local economic driver of its own rather than digital colony of the US. Internet has become a critical element of China's economic progress in the past five years, accounting for seven percent of the nation's gross domestic product (GDP) in 2014, a percentage point higher than the US. The Chinese characteristics of e-commerce are inclusion, efficiency and innovation.

It promotes inclusion of firms in the world economy by enabling more firms to trade new products to newer destinations. For instance, firms selling their goods online through Alibaba, China's leading e-commerce company, are smaller and younger and export more products to different destinations than firms selling offline. Alibaba's B2B trading platform helped small businesses (suppliers and manufactures in China) to connect with buyers in North America and Europe. It raises efficiency by allowing firms to make better use of their capital and labour. For instance, real-time data help equipment manufacturers in China turn over their inventory stocks five times faster than suppliers not connected to the internet. It enhances innovation by enabling firms to exploit scale effects through online platforms and services that compete with conventional business models.

Successful online platforms cannot necessarily be transplanted to a foreign country without adapting to the local market and institutions. The entry of eBay into China illustrates this. Both eBay and Taobao, Alibaba's consumer-to-consumer (C2C) platform, entered the Chinese market in 2003 and established their dominant market share of 85 percent by acquiring Chinese market leader, Each Net a But. Taobao took the dominant position and by 2014, it accounted for over 80 percent of the Chinese C2C market (eBay exited the Chinese market in 2006).

Alibaba's success can be explained by its ability to adapt to local market conditions and culture to remove the information asymmetries unique to the Chinese C2C market. The Taobao website, for instance, indicates whether sellers are online and allows buyers to communicate instantly with the sellers through an online messaging system. Alibaba further guarantees foreign buyers in timely delivery of their money and implemented a system to verify sellers on its website for business-to-business (B2B) transactions.

Chinese internet companies had put emphasis on innovation led growth and have been innovating at the intersection of mobile, social and commerce and had created valuable businesses. The success of China's internet companies can be attributed to blocking many Western services in the country. China is an example of a country where businesses can become a global leader without selling outside its domestic market. With 674 million internet users, the sheer size of China's consumer market means many domestic companies command a huge global market share. The scale of China's digital market means it will remain core to its local firms.

A number of provinces have developed portals with

agricultural information including pricing and the ability to advertise products with offline purchases. Some have also implemented B2B initiatives such as farmers pooling purchases to achieve scale for buying inputs such as fertilizers. Rural e-commerce have often emanated from the ground up, as in the case in the rural Jiangsu and Zhejiang provinces. In China, rural e-commerce has been more grassroots driven, but supported indirectly by local governments.

The Government's contribution to the development of rural e-commerce in China included tax breaks, preferential loans and construction of distribution warehouses.

The telecommunications regulations of the People's Republic of China stipulated the Ministry of Industry and Information Technology to be the governing body for electronic commerce. Further in 2004, China adopted the Electronic Signature Law, which is widely recognized as the first law in Chinese e-commerce legislation. This law is considered a milestone in the regulation and propagation of Chinese e-commerce, and is one of the reasons for its rapid ascent in the global e-commerce scenario. Government regulations resulted in most foreign companies partnering with local players. For example, e-commerce related licenses are rarely granted to multinationals, leading them to form joint ventures with local partners as minority shareholders. Therefore, multinationals have realized "in China for China" strategy.

15.6 Summing Up

In India, Digital India mission has gone into a buffering mode. Companies such as Flipkart and Snapdeal's long-term profitability in the country, is still under question. After so many years of operations, all the major e-retailers are yet to start making profits. Global rivals such as Amazon and Uber are much bigger in terms of size and capital, and are able to deploy cash and technology from the US into India.

All these companies are closely held companies and are not made public, hence their valuation is a difficult task. As there are no credible figures, valuation is done through demand and supply of stock. Also, in growth stage, one can look into financial matrices like gross margin, profit after tax, earnings before interest, taxes,depreciation and amortization.

The low internet penetration and limited awareness and educational levels among the poor are obstructing widespread adoption. Personal computers and internet require literacy and often foreign language (especially English) skills. Computers with internet capabilities in the Warana sub-district in Maharashtra went largely unused except for transmitting market information to farmers, a function later substituted by mobile phones, which were cheaper and easier to use.

E-commerce in India is governed by the Information and Technology Act of 2000. This blanket Act is meant to cover all aspects of cyber law and electronic commerce, including cyber stalking, child pornography, hacking, cracking, and network trespassing. There is no specific law governing e-commerce in India. The Competition Commission of India is the sole regulator for all markets in India including the e-commerce market.

It is not that India cannot catch up with China, it is just that China is an early starter. The success of Alibaba in China may be replicated in India only if home-grown companies such as Flipkart, Snapdeal, etc. focus on, 'in India, for India', that is, customize the requirements according to local language, culture, and local content, instead of following the Western countries. Companies should understand that India is a vast country with diverse culture and if e-commerce companies cater to customers in their own language and culture, they can reap the benefits of scale economies.

It is not only the Alibaba but also Government in China had played a positive role in reducing rural-urban divide and promoting e-commerce in rural areas. Government in India like in China should also devise policy to encourage the growth of e-commerce beyond metros and tier-2 cities.

Since valuation of services is difficult, therefore, black economy had concentrated in the services sector and hence difficulties in taxation of the service sector. Further, with the growth of e-commerce, the difficulty of taxing e-commerce is more. From experiences of US and EU, it is clear that taxing e-commerce is something that governments are trying but are not able to settle down and in the US, the data seems to indicate that there is loss of revenue.

Although, internet and e-commerce have been expanding worldwide since the 1990s, yet India had been a late starter, hence there is a need to learn from the experiences of other countries. It is useful to learn from China's Alibaba, as to how it had grown rapidly and its approach of an all inclusive growth.

Even though India is supposed to be software super power, nonetheless, the activity of e-commerce started very late and instead of devising our own model like China did, we followed what was done in the West and therefore were not able to reap the benefits compared to China.

We have borrowed and copied the model from the West, but it had not proved beneficial. We can borrow the idea from the West and tailor it to our requirements in terms of infrastructure, language, culture.

Taxation of services has been difficult due to its high buoyancy. Undoubtedly, if the penetration would have been higher, the problem of taxing services would have been lesser and more revenue could have been generated. The internet divide in the country is mainly due to infrastructural issues. The country should follow a policy of expanding infrastructure, so that e-commerce could expand rapidly and can benefit a vast majority of the population.

Given the cultural and linguistic diversification in India, localized online content and customized e-commerce services is a significant opportunity to enhance online buying experience. Government should implement policies that enable and nurture local digital talent.

Although, e-commerce would appear to be desirable and more efficient due to economies of scale, since it reduces cost of storage and transportation etc., yet, on the other hand, it may also lead to problems of unemployment since a lot of small traders may be hit. Due to internet penetration, e-commerce is yet to pick up momentum in rural areas.

References/Bibliography

References/Bibliography

Agrawal, Rajat (2014), "Flipkart Raises $ 210 Million in Financing Round Led by DST Global", BGR.in, May 26, 2014.

Agarwal, Sapna (2013), "Around 60% of Jabong.com's Revenue Comes from Small Towns", Medianama, September 3, 2013.

Ahuja, Astha (2004), "Value Added Tax: Indian and Global Experiences, New Delhi: New Century Publications.

Asthana, Shishir (2014), "All You Want to Know about Amazon India's Tax Issue", *Business Standard*, September 17, 2014.

Asthana, Shishir (2016), "Flipkart Opposes Entry Tax by States: Why it is a Fight to the Finish", *Business Standard*, March 16, 2016.

Atkinson, A.B. (1991), "Modern Public Finance", *International Library of Critical Writings in Economics*, No. 15, England: Elgars.

Atkinson, A.B. (1981), "On the Switch to Indirect Taxation", London School of Economics and Political Science, Social Science Research Council Programme.

Atkinson, A.B. and Stern, N.H. (1980), "On the Switch from Direct to Indirect Taxation", London School of Economics and Political Science, *Journal of Public Economics*, Vol. 14(3), October.

Atkinson, A.B. and Stiglitz, J.E. (1991), "The Design of Tax Structure: Direct Indirect Taxation", 'Modern Public Finance', Vol. 2, Atkinson, A.B. (ed.), *International Library of Critical Writings in Economics*, No. 15, England: Elgar.

Bajwa, Gurshaminder Singh (n.d.), "ICT Policy in India in the Era of Liberalisation: Its Impact and Consequences", *GBER*, Vol. 3, No. 2, pp. 49-61.

Baller, Silja (2016), "The Global Information Technology Report: Innovating in the Digital Economy", World Economic Forum.

Balanarayan, N.T. (2014), "Jabong Reports 1.95M Orders, 0.79M Transacting Customers for Q1 2014", available at: http://www.medianama.com/2014/05/223-jabong-reports-1-95m-orders-0-79m-transacting-customers-for-q1-2014.

Balakrishnan, Reghu (2014), "Discounts Backfire: Many E-com Ventures Shut Shop", *Business Standard*, February 26, 2014.

Ballay Rasul (2016), "Flipkart, Amazon Losing Crores Due to UP Tax Rule", *Times of India*, January 15, 2016.

Banga, Rashmi (2005), "Critical Issues in India's Service-Led Growth", ICRIER Working Paper No. 171, October.

Basu, S. (2001), "Taxation of Electronic Commerce", *The Journal of Information, Law and Technology (JILT)*, available at: http://elj.warwick.ac.uk/jilt/01-2/basu1.html.

Basu, Subhajit (2003), "Relevance of E-Commerce for Taxation: An Overview", *Global Jurist Topics,* Vol. 3, Issue 3.

Basu, Subhajit and Jones, Richard (2001), "Taxation of Electronic Commerce: A Developing Problem", 16th BILETA Annual Conference, available at: http://www.bileta.ac.uk/01papers/rjones.html.

Bird, Richard M. (1992), "Tax Policy and Economic Development", John Hopkins Studies in Development, London: John Hopkins University Press.

Browntape (2015), "India and China in E-commerce: Rise of the New Frontiers", October 23, 2015, blog.

Blystone, Da (2015), "Alibaba's Business Model", *Investopedia*, June 23.

Caberwal, Sonny (2011), "4 Reasons E-commerce is Set to Boom in India", *Exclusively.in*, March 30.

Camburn, Weaver Mike and Tim Dümichen, Brett A. (2013), "E-commerce: Tax in the Digital Domain", EMA Tax Summit, KPMG.

Chaffery, Dave (2011), "8 Online Revenue Model Options for Internet Businesses", *Smart Insights*, January 10, available at: www.smartinsights.co.uk.

Chatterjee, Paramita (2012), "Snapdeal Acquires Esportsbuy.com", *The Economic Times*, April 4.

Chaudhary, Apurva (2013), "Jabong Goes International with Jabongworld.com", *Medianama*, February 4.

Chissick, M. and Kelman, A. (2000), "Electronic Commerce Law and Practice", 2nd edition.

Cho, Janet H. (2015), "Ohio Retailers Elated that Amazon.com Will Collect Sales Tax Starting Monday", *The Plain Dealer* , May 29.

Choudhury,Varnana (2015), "What is GST? And What Could be Its Impact on the Indian E-commerce Avenue", *Wire*, May 7.

CII (2016), "E-commerce in India: A Game Changer for the Economy", April.

Cnosse, Sijbern (1997), "Recent Developments in Excise and Sales Taxation", *Bulletin for International Fiscal Documentation*, Vol. 31(10).

Dahlman, C.J. (2007), "China and India: Emerging Technological Powers", *Issues in Science and Technology*, 23(3), pp. 45-53.

Dalal, Mihir and Verma, Shrutika (2014), "How Flipkart, Amazon and Snapdeal Fund Discounts", *Live Mint*, October 21.

Dalal, Mihir and Verma, Shrutika (2015), "Snapdeal Buys E-commerce Management Firm Uni Commerce", *Live Mint*, March 31.

Dalal, Mihir and Verma, Shrutika (2015), "India's E-commerce Frenzy", *Live Mint*, April 17.

Dalal, Mihir and Mishra, Asit Ranjan (2016), "Government Defines E-commerce Marketplace Rules, Allows 100% FDI", *Live Mint*, March 30.

Dalal, Mihir (2016), "India's E-commerce Boom", *Live Mint*, July 13.

Deaton, Angus S. (1979), "Optimally Uniform Commodity Taxes", *Economics Letters*.

Dhanya, Ann Thoppil (2014), "India;s Flipkart Raises $1 Billion in Fresh Funding", July 29, available at:
wsj.com.

Dhanya, Ann Thoppil (2015), "India's Snapdeal Buys FreeCharge", *The Wall Street Journal*, April 8.

Dharma Kumar, Rohin (2011), "E-Commerce In India", *Forbes India*, July 25.

Due, John F. (1986), "A Brief Summary of Excise and Sales Taxation in India", University of Illinois at Urban-Campaign, Bureau of Economics and Business Research faculty paper, January.

Ernst and Young (2012), "Rebirth of E-commerce in India", available at:
www.ey.com.

Garg, Neha (2016), "Alibaba: The World's Greatest Bazaar", *International Journal of Management and Social Sciences Research (IJMSSR)*, Vol. 5, No. 1, January.

Gilbert, Alorie (2004), "E-Commerce Turns 10", *CNET News*, August.

Goolsbee, Austan (2000), "In a World Without Borders: The Impact of Taxes on Internet Commerce", *The Quarterly Journal of*

Economics, Vol. 115, Issue 2, pp. 561-576.

Gooptu, Biswarup (2014), "eBay Increases Stake in Snapdeal, Invests $134 Million", *The Economic Times*, February 27, available at: articles.economictimes.indiatimes.com.

Gooptu, Biswarup (2015), "Snapdeal Acquires Majority Stake of RupeePower", April 1, available at: articles.economictimes.indiatimes.com.

Gooptu, Biswarup (2015), "Snapdeal Acquires Silicon Valley Start-up Reduce Data", *The Economic Times*, September 2, available at: articles.economictimes.indiatimes.com.

Gooptu, Biswarup, Shrivastava, Aditi and Aulakh, Gulveen (2015), "Flipkart Begins Preparations for another Round of Funding to Raise Rs. 10,500 Crore", *The Economic Times*, February 17.

Gordon, James and Guta, Poonam (2004), "Understanding India's Services Revolution", IMF Working Paper WP/04/171, September.

Gordon, James P.F. (1989), "Tax Reform via Commodity Grouping", *Journal of Public Economics*, June.

Government of India, Ministry of Finance, "Budget Speech of the Finance Minister, 2001-2002", Part B, p. 26.

Government of India, Ministry of Finance, "Report of the Indirect Taxation Enquiry Committee (Chairman: L.K. Jha)", 1977.

Government of India, Ministry of Finance, "Report of the Taxation Enquiry Commission (Chairman: John Matthai), 1953-54", Vol. II, p. 519.

Guilford, Gwynn (2014), "Alibaba Has a New Way of Explaining Its Controversial Alipay Spinoff", *Quartz,* June 16.

Gulati, Sonam (2012), "Jabong Bangs into Top Rung of Indian E-commerce: Can it Sustain?", *TechCircle.com,* August 1.

Gulati, Sonam (2013), "Excl: Jabong comes Up with Managed Marketplace to Expand it this Year", *TechCircle.com,* May 10.

Gulati V.P.,Ganpathy, K.R. and Saxena, Ashutosh (n.d.), "Electronic Commerce and Banks in India", IDRBT's Working Paper No. 3. Institute for Development and Research in Banking Technology.

Gupte, Medha, J. (2015), "Growth of the Service Sector in India: What Does it Augur for the Future", *International Journal of Research in Business Management*, Vol. 3, Issue 1, January.

Hansda, Sanjay K. (2002), "Services Sector in the Indian Growth

Process: Myths and Realities", *The Journal of Income and Wealth,* Vol. 24, No. 1 and 2, January-December.

Hatzipanayotou, Panos, Michael, Micheals and Miller, Stephen M. (1994), "Win-Win Indirect Tax Reform: A Modest Proposal", *Economics Letters*, Vol. 44, 1-2.

Hector, Darlington Jose (2013), "Jabbing its Way to the Top", *The Financial Express*, October 14.

Huenink, Douglas (2013), "Eliminating the E-commerce Sales Tax: Advantage in the United States by Following in the Footsteps of the European Union", *Wisconsin International Law Journal.*

Eurogroup Consulting (2012), "How Product Brands Integrate Online Sales in their Supply Chain the Effects of E-commerce on the Supply Chain".

Jain, Vimal (2015), "Online Service Providers like Flipkart are not Liable to VAT", November 17, available at: www.caclubindia.com/articles/online-service-providers-like-flipkart-are-not-liable-to-vat-25449.asp.

Jayadevan, P.K. (n.d.), "Flipkart Raises Fresh $200 mn from Existing Investors Tiger Global, Naspers and Others", NextBigWhat.

JLL (Jones Lang LaSalle's) (2013), "E-commerce Boom Triggers Transformation in Retail Logistics", November.

Kabongo, Mbayo (2015), "Factors Influencing E-commerce Development: Implications for the Developing Countries", *International Journal of Innovation and Economic Development*, Vol. 1, Issue 1, April, pp. 59-66.

Khedekar, Naina (2014), "Learn from the Master: Alibaba Shows Flipkart, Snapdeal What it Takes to Pull off a Sale", *First Post,* November 12.

Kumar, Arun (1988), "Budget 1988-89: Diminishing Returns of Unchanged Fiscal Policy Regime", *Economic and Political Weekly*, April 2-9.

Kumar, A. (1988), "The Black Economy, Services and Surplus: The Growing Triad", Centre for Economic Studies and Planning, School of Social Sciences, New Delhi: Jawaharlal Nehru University.

Kumar, Arun (1996), "Union Budget 1996-97: Reaching the Limits of Resource Mobilisation under Market Conditions, *Economic and Political Weekly*, September 21.

Kumar, Arun (2005), "The Flawed Macro Statistics: Over Estimated Growth and Under Estimated Inflation", *Alternative Economic*

Survey of India, 2005-2006.

Kumar, Pradeep J. and Panchanatham, N. (2010), "A Study on Impact of Rural College Students in E-learning (Nagapattinam District, Tamilnadu)", *Perspectives of Innovations, Economics and Business*, 4(1), pp. 98-102.

Loiacono, Eleanor T. (2005), "A Cross-Cultural Comparison of U.S. and Chinese Website Customers", *Journal of International Technology and Information Management*, Vol. 14, Issue 1.

Mazerov, Michael (1998), "Federal Moratorium on Internet Commerce Taxes Would Erode State and Local Revenues and Shift Burdens to Lower Income Household", Center on Budget and Policy Priorities, June, 19, available at: http://www.cbtp.org/512webtax.html#III.A moratorium taxation.

Mazerov, Michael (2003), "Expanding Sales Taxation of Services: Options and Issues", Center on Budget and Policy Priorities, Washington, D.C., June 19.

McKinsey & Company (2007), "The Bird of Gold: The Rise of India's Consumer Market", May.

Mishra, Digbijay (2014), "Jabong's Revenue Rose 50 Times in FY13", *Business Standard*, November 22, available at: www.businessstandard.com.

Mishra, Digbijay, Viveat, Susan Pinto and Pathak, Kalpana (2014), "Are E-commerce Valuations Sustainable?", *Business Standard*, December 1.

Mookerji, Nivedita and Soni, Anusha (2014), "Why Are E-retailers Indifferent to Profit?", *Business Standard*, June 10, available at: www.businessstandard.com.

Monahan, M., Shah, A. and Rana, J. (2015), "E-commerce on the Subcontinent: How Indian Consumers Will Shape Demand", *Journal of International Business and Cultural Studies*, Vol. 9, January.

Mukherjee, Debashish (2016), "FDI in E-commerce: Who are We Protecting?", *Live Mint*, April 22.

Nayyar, Dhiraj (2015), "Beware India's E-Commerce Bubble", *Bloomberg View*, May 7.

Pachisia,Vivek (n.d.), "GST Could be Key to Unlock Issues Faced by E-commerce Sector", available at: www.ey.com.

Pahwa, Nikhil (2011), "Distribution of Music, E-books, Games", *Medianama*, October 11.

Panagariya, Arvind (2000), "E-commerce, WTO and Developing Countries", United Nations Conference on Trade and Development, Policy Issues in International Trade and Commodities Study Series No. 2, available at: unctad.org/en/Docs/itcdtab3_en.pdf.

Parikh, Vinish (2014), "Difference between Online Shopping and Physical Shopping", *Lets Learn Finance*, November 23.

Peer, Nikita (2015), "Snapdeal Buys Stake in Product Comparison Site Smartprix.com", *VC Circle*, January 5.

Pitt, L.F., Berthon, P.R. and Berthon, J.P. (1999), "Changing Channels: The Impact of the Internet on Distribution Strategy", *Business Horizons*, 42, 2, March- April.

Prabhudesai, Arun (2014), "Flipkart Vs. Amazon Vs. Snapdeal: Revenues and Losses Comparison", *Trak.in*, posted in E-Commerce, November 6.

Prasad, Gireesh Chandra (2015), "Flipkart, Snapdeal, Others in Line of Fire as E-trade Tax Near Top of States' Budget Wishlist, *The Financial Express*, February 12.

Rai, Archana (2010), "Flipkart: Country's Largest Online Book Store", *The Economic Times*.

Relph, M. (2011), "India's Online Shopping Spree", *Time,* 178, (23), pp. B1-B2.

Ranjan, Smruti (2013), "Must Haves for 2013 by Jabong.com", *Right Column Media,* January 7.

Rau, Amrish B. (2012), "E-commerce: A Boon for the Current Economic Downturn", First Data India and ICICI Merchant.

Reardon, Marguerite (2013), "Confused About Online Sales Taxes? You're Not Alone", CNET, December 4.

Report of the Indirect Taxation Enquiry Committee, 1977, Part I, op. cit., p. 49.

Reuters (2016), "India Approves Foreign Investment in E-commerce", March 30.

Sachitanand, Rahul (2013), "How Flipkart's Sachin and Binny Bansal Revolutionised E-commerce in India", *The Economic Times*, December 6, available at: www.economictimes.com.

Satnalika, Niraj (2012), "Issues of the Indian Service Sector: Classification of Services, GDP, Outsourcing and Growth Rate", *Green World Investor*, December 6.

Saxena, Gopal (2015), "Legal and Taxation Issues Concerning E-commerce", *The Indian Journal of Law and Technology*, Vol. 11.

Sen, Chitrakalpa (2011), "FDI in the Service Sector: Propagator of Growth for India?", G.D. Goenka World Institute, Gurgaon, India, April 18.

Sharma, Itika (2014), "Flipkart Co-founders Apologise for Glitches", *Business Standard.com*, October 8.

Sharma, Samidha (2013), "Nearly 16 Million Log on to 4-day Online Shopping Festival", *The Times of India*, December 25, available at:
Shoppingnavigator.co.uk.

Singh, Didar (2002), "Electronic Commerce: Issues of Policy and Strategy for India", Working Paper No. 86, ICRIER (Indian Council for Research on International Economic Relations).

Singh, Shelly (2016), "E-commerce Firms Brace for Life without Discounts", *The Economic Times*, July 12.

Tun, ZawThiha (2015), "How Counterfeiting Affects Alibaba's Business", *Investopedia*, June 23.

Ueland, Sig (2014), "13 Deal Sites for E-commerce Merchants", *Practical E-Commerce*, June 9, available at:
www.practicalecommerce.com/articles/69111-13-Deal-Sites-for-Ecommerce-Merchants.

UK Essays (2015), "The Alibaba Group Company Analysis", March 23.

UK Essays (2015), "Market Analysis and Strategy for Alibaba", March 23.

Vaitheeswaran, K. (2016), "FDI in E-commerce: No More Fifty Shades of Grey", *Your Story*, March 31, available at:
www.yourstory.com.

Vardaan, B. (2015), "Flipkart Acquires US-Based Startup Appiterate", *IndianWeb2*, April 29.

Vardhan, Jai (2015), "Flipkart Acquires Global Mobile Ad Network Adiquity to Boost New Revenue Channels", *Your Story*, March 7.

Vardhan, Jai (2015), "RBI Approves Payments License to Airtel, Paytm", *Your Story*, August 19, available at:
https://yourstory.com/2015/08/rbi-approves-payments-bank-license.

Varun, Sumangla (2015), "Can India Catch up to E-commerce in China?", *Indianonlineseller.com*, August 22.

Verma, Shrutika (2015), "Snapdeal Acquired 20% Stake in Gojavas.com", *Live Mint,* March 19.

Vikas, S.N. (2014), "Jabong Posts Rs. 293.4 Cr loss in FY14; Net Revenue Up 3x to Rs. 438.6 Cr.", *Medianama*, October 9, available at: http://www.medianama.com/2014/10/223-jabong-fy14-earnings.

Vikas, S.N. (2013), "Flipkart Raises $160M from Dragoneer Investment", Morgan Stanley Investment and Others, *Medianama*, October 9.

Williams, Mark (2015), "Amazon to Start Collecting Sales Tax on Ohioans' Purchases", *The Columbus Dispatch*, May 29.

World Development Report, 2016.

WTO (2004), "E-commerce and Information Technologies: World Trade, available at: https://www.wto.org/english/tratop_e/serv_e/sym_april05_e/wunschvincent_e.pd fby S Wunsch-Vincent.

Yadav, Manoj (2015), "Success of Online Shopping Portals: An Overview", available at: http://blog.mobiloitte.com/success-online-shopping-portals-overview.

Youderian, Andrew (2014), "Alibaba vs. Amazon: An In-Depth Comparison of Two E-commerce Giants", October 24.

Index

Index

K

L

M

N

O

P

R

S

T